Join the Dots and Colouring

CULTURAL MASKS FROM AROUND THE WORLD

First published in 2020.
Copy writing and editing by Ben Korda.
Cover design by Omar Coloma and Ben Korda.
Artwork by Ben Korda, Omar Coloma and Pedro Viteri.

Disclaimer:

All artwork and design in this book is original.

Any resemblance to exisiting masks, pictures or patterns is purely coincidental.

Every effort has been made to correctly research the origin country of these masks.

All rights are reserved. No portion of this book may be reproduced in any form without permission from the author.

References:

"freevectormaps.com" - https://freevectormaps.com/world-maps/WRLD-EPS-02-0012?ref=atr

"Hannya in Japanese Folklore" - https://suzannalinton.com/

"International Carnival and Mask Museum Binche" - http://museebinche.be/

"masksoftheworld.com" - https://masksoftheworld.com/

"Museum of Cultural Masks" - https://www.maskmuseum.org/

"The Mask Museum of San Miguel de Allende" - https://www.maskmuseumsma.com/index.html

"The real man in the Iron mask" - https://www.livescience.com/

Permissions and Contact:

For permissions please contact Ben Korda at benkorda@gmail.com

The cultural importance of masks

Masks have made an appearance in almost every culture and civilization in the world both past and present. Some masks are used for religious, territorial, celebratory, medicinal and protective purposes and in some cultures, it is believed that masks can even stimulate one's fertility while in other cultures masks are used to scare children into behaving. There are so many uses for masks; it would take multiple weighty books to even come close to describing their rich cultural and historical significance.

Secret societies use masks to protect individuals' identities and to help identify each other. The ancient Greek playwrights used their exaggerated expressions to show a character's true nature and allow males to play female roles; Shamans use masks to help distance themselves from the outside world in order to reach a trance like state and scare away evil spirits.

Masks have solidified their place in folklore and are often the subject of stories from those told around the campfire to Hollywood blockbusters such as "The Man in the Iron Mask" starring Leonardo Dicaprio and John Malkovich. In the movie adaptation of The Man in the Iron Mask the identical twin sons of King Louis XIII were split at birth to avoid a potentially violent duel claim to the throne. Queen Anne, the mother, was then told that one of her children had died at birth. The supposedly dead son was hidden away unaware of his claim to the throne of France while his twin brother was prepared for his future role as King. When the future king learnt of his brother's existence, he found him, imprisoned him and forced him to wear a mask to conceal his identity. They based the film on the story of a man who was imprisoned in the Bastille in Paris. Many historians are in agreement that the prisoner wore a mask on occasion but it was more likely velvet, not iron. This shows that even the gentle and soft material of a mask can be evolved to a cruelly uncomfortable one to create an iconic legend.

The designs of masks often prove to be just as intricate as their origin stories, a wonderful example of this is the Japanese Hannya mask. One of its origin stories, despite being rather misogynistic is nevertheless an entertaining tale in which a woman is betrayed by her partner and becomes so enraged that she turns into a demon. The mask not only depicts a twisted, angry expression but also a confused and heartbroken one. This intricate mask is therefore able to display the diverse array of emotions that she feels and as a result it has become world famous.

With the recent COVID-19 pandemic masks have become common place around the world. These masks are certainly a far cry from the traditional masks featured in this book, but they are quickly becoming cultural symbols. People are using them to express their own individuality with unique designs, and they are even being used for commentary on our ever-changing political landscape. Perhaps these modern masks of protection draw inspiration from the past. Either way it is clear that masks are deeply rooted in culture and history.

Contents

- 7 • Aya Huma Mask (Ecuador)
- 9 • Bedu Mask (Ivory Coast)
- 11 • Brunca Devil Mask (Costa Rica)
- 13 • Bwa Mask (Burkina Faso)
- 15 • Cheoyongmu Mask (Korea)
- 17 • Dancing Devil Mask (Venezuela)
- 19 • Dayak Mask (Borneo)
- 21 • Day of the Dead Mask (Mexico)
- 23 • Dionysus Mask (Greece)
- 25 • Garuda Mask (India)
- 27 • Guro Antelope Mask (Ivory Coast)
- 29 • Hannya Mask (Japan)
- 31 • Hanuman Mask (Indonesia)
- 33 • Kali Mask (India)
- 35 • Kamayura Mask (Brazil)
- 37 • Maori Mask (New Zealand)
- 39 • Mikishi Mask (DR Congo)
- 41 • Monkey Mask (Ecuador)
- 43 • Monkey Mask (Japan)
- 45 • Namahage Mask (Japan)
- 47 • NWC Mask (Canada)
- 49 • Opera Mask (China)
- 51 • Owl Mask (Burkina Faso)
- 53 • Pre-Columbian Mask (Mexico)
- 55 • Rangda Mask (Bali, Indonesia)
- 57 • Tapuanu Mask (Micronesia)
- 59 • Tiger Mask (Mexico)
- 61 • Tin Mask (Mexico)
- 63 • Venetian Mask (Italy)
- 65 • Warrior Mask (Kenya)

Aya Huma Mask
Ecuador

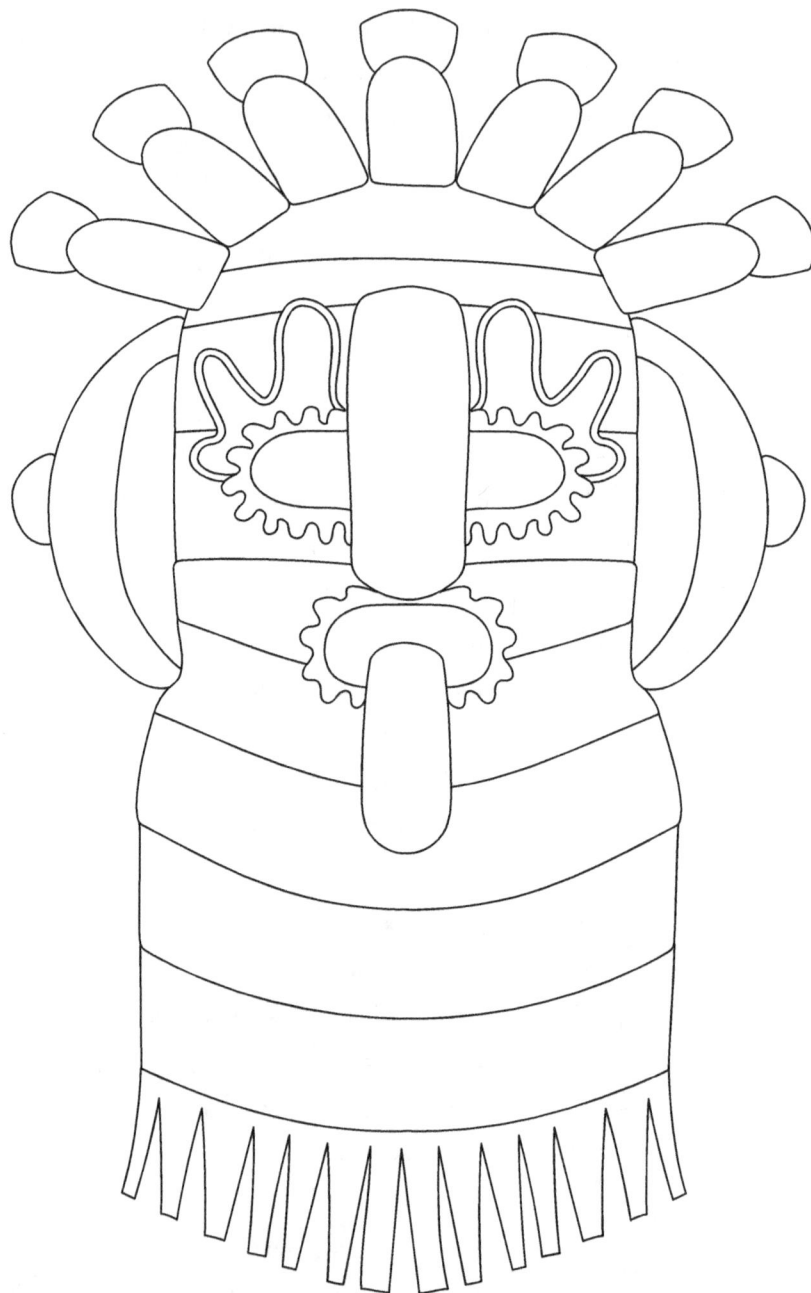

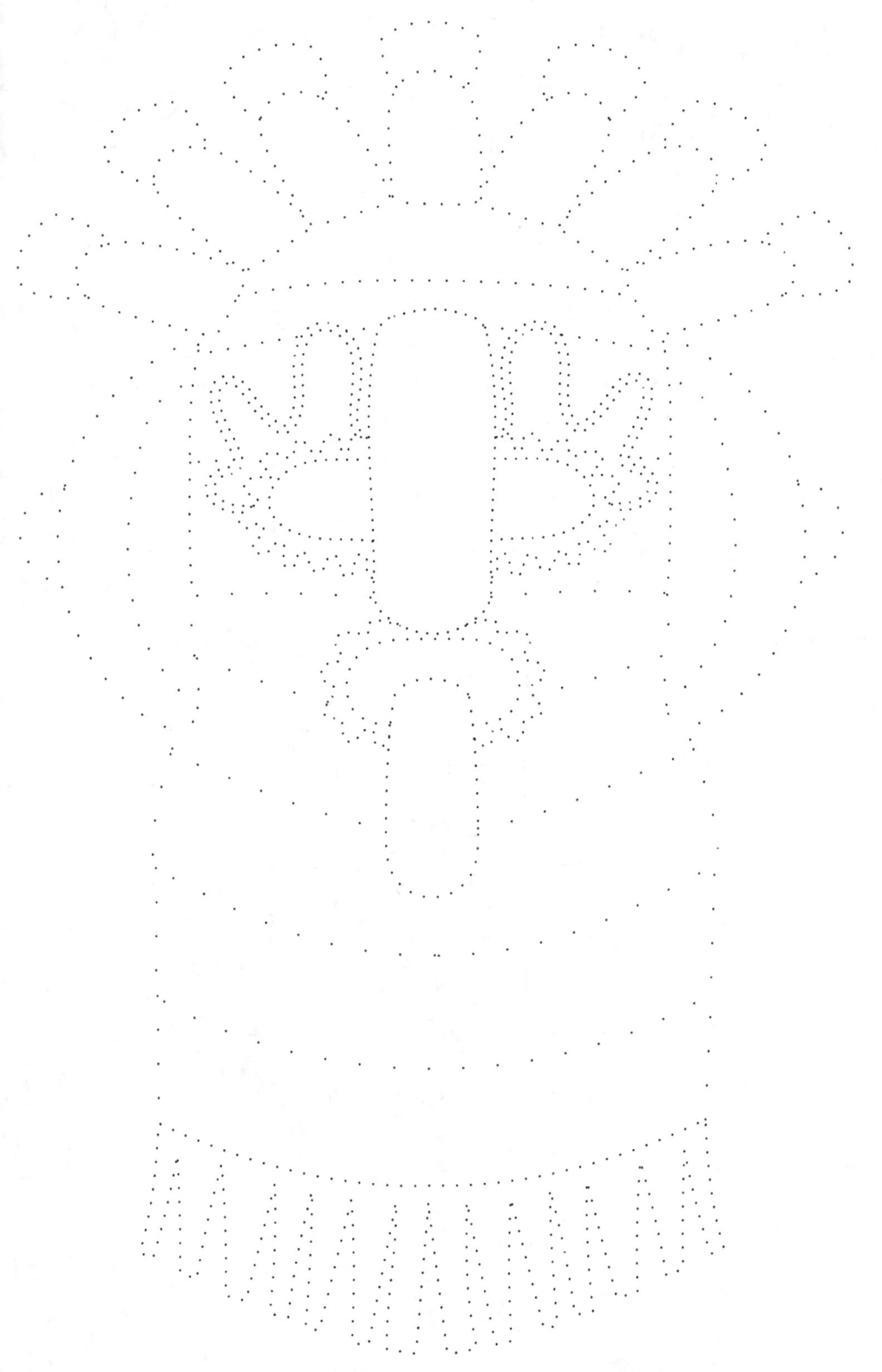

Bedu Mask

Ivory Coast

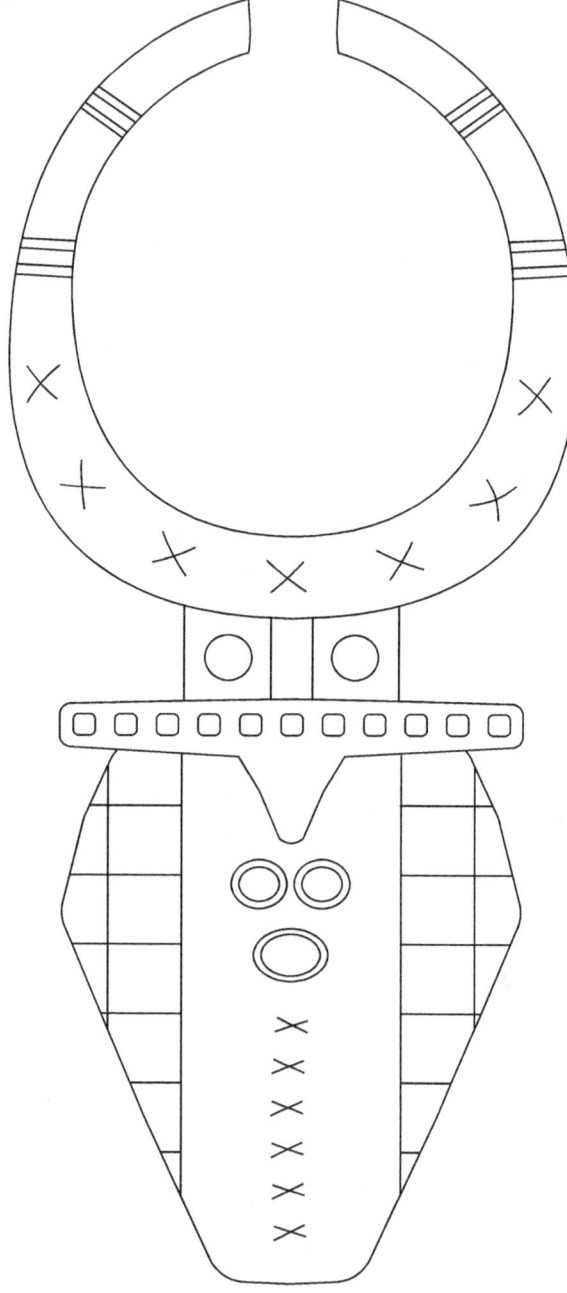

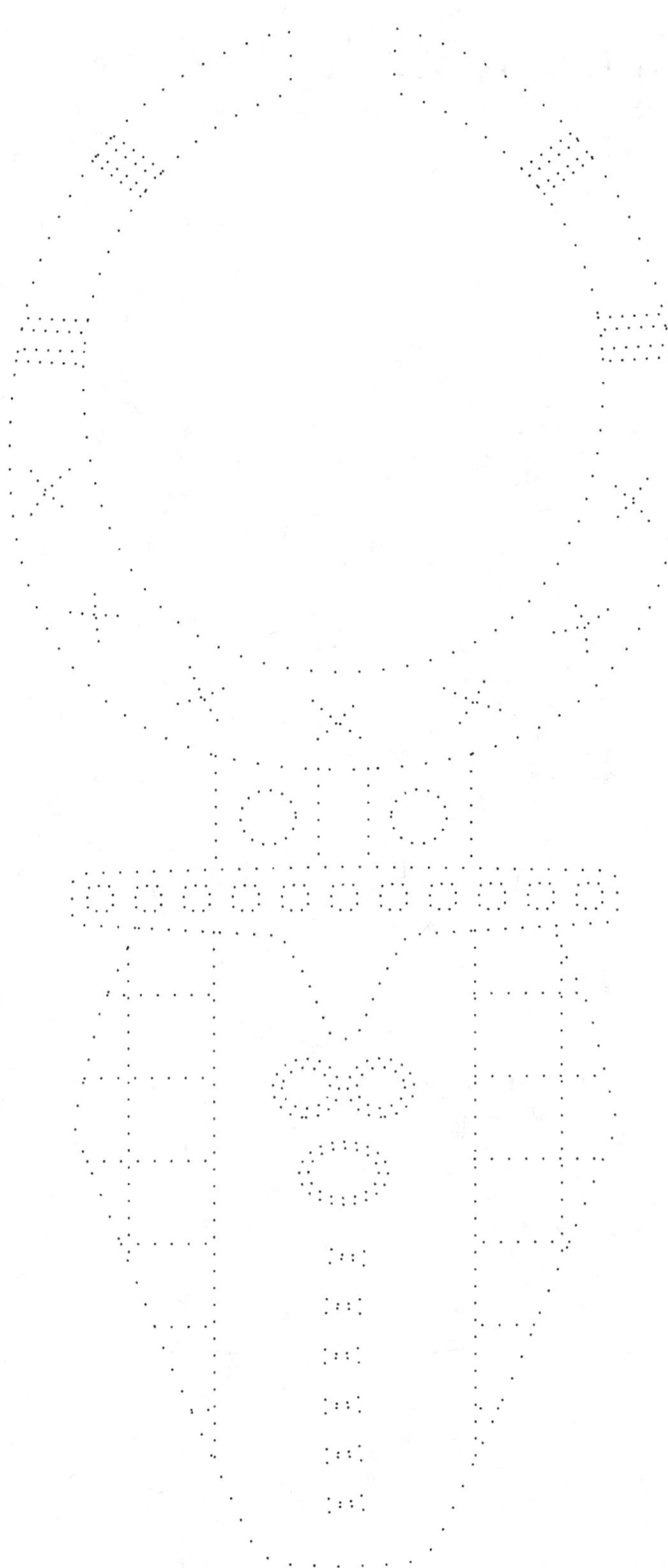

Brunca Devil Mask

Costa Rica

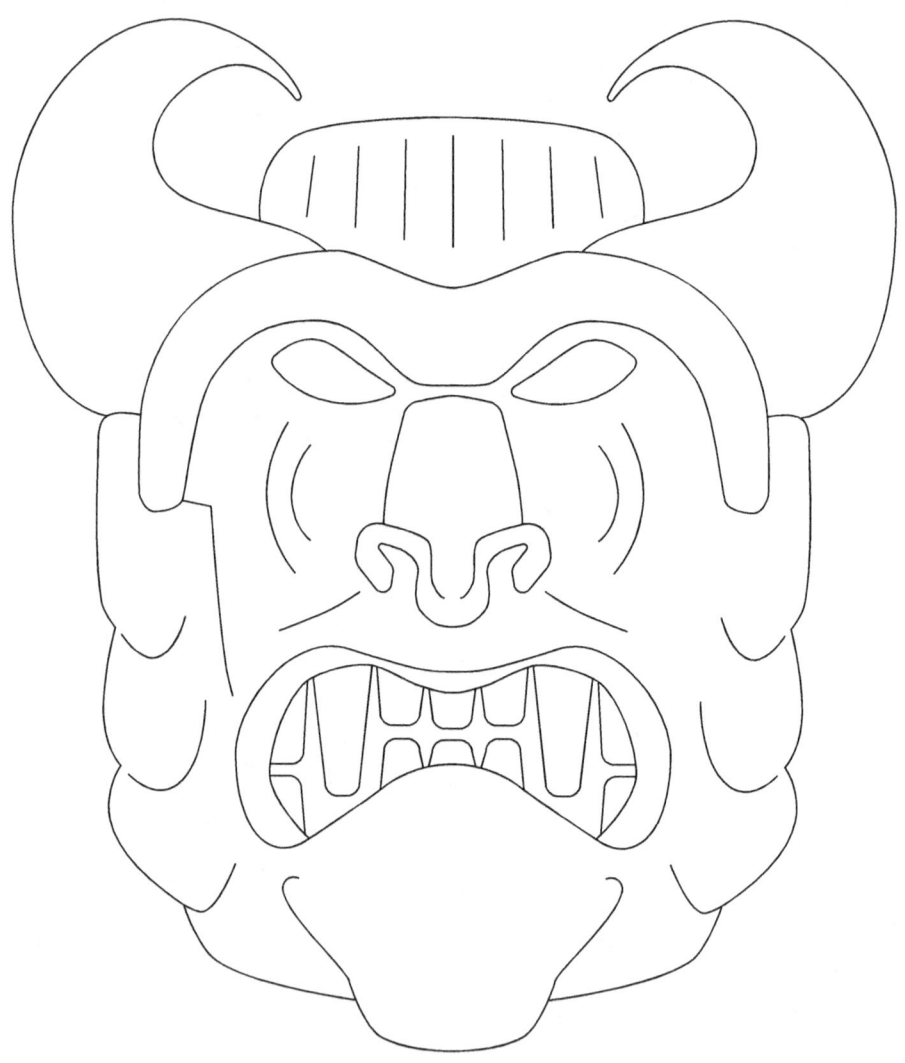

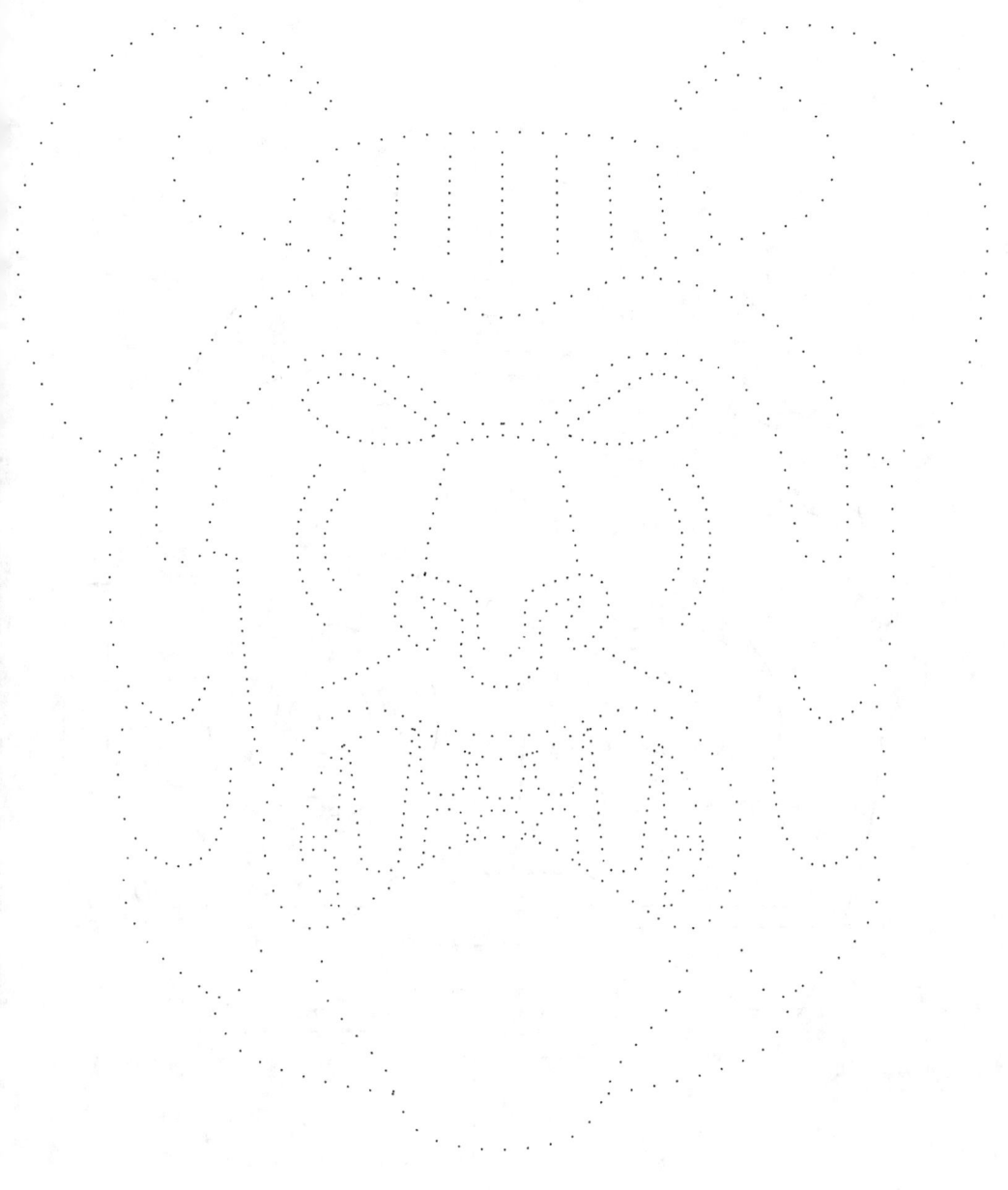

Bwa Mask
Burkina Faso

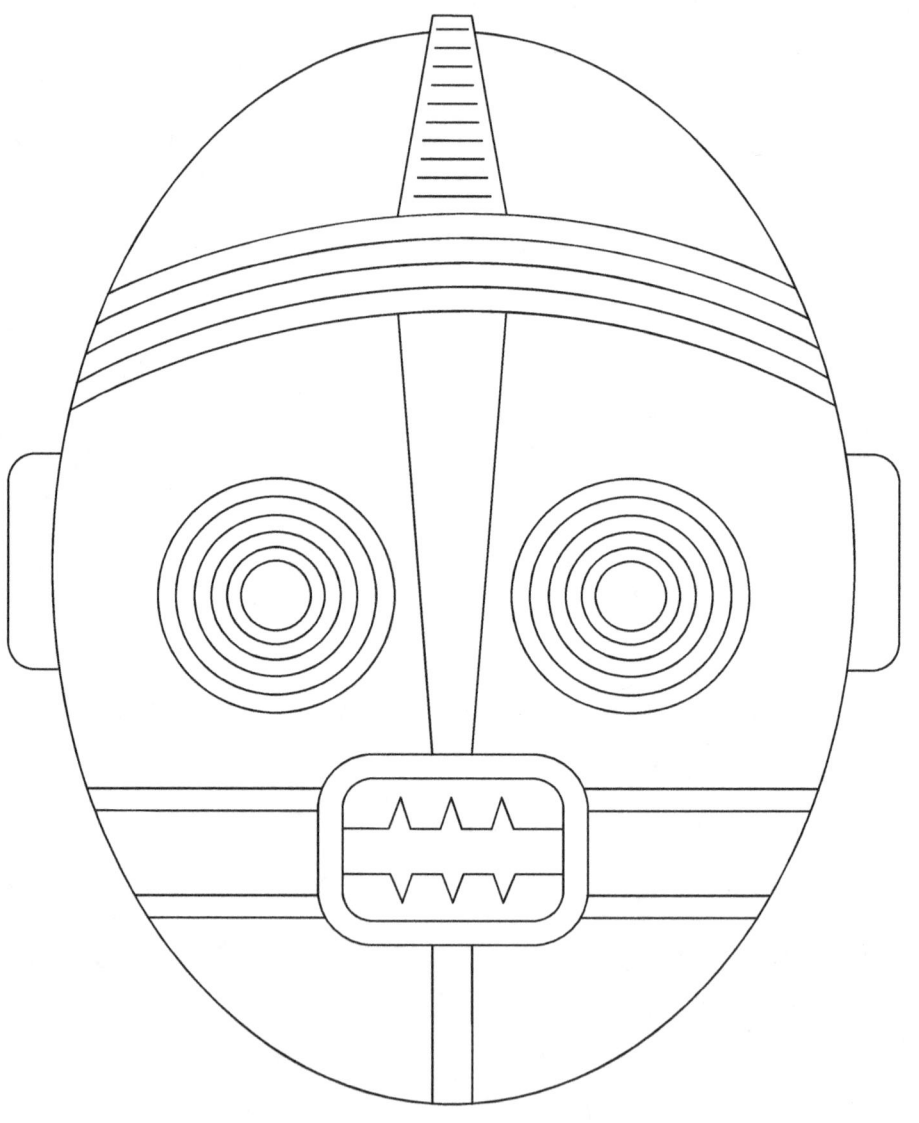

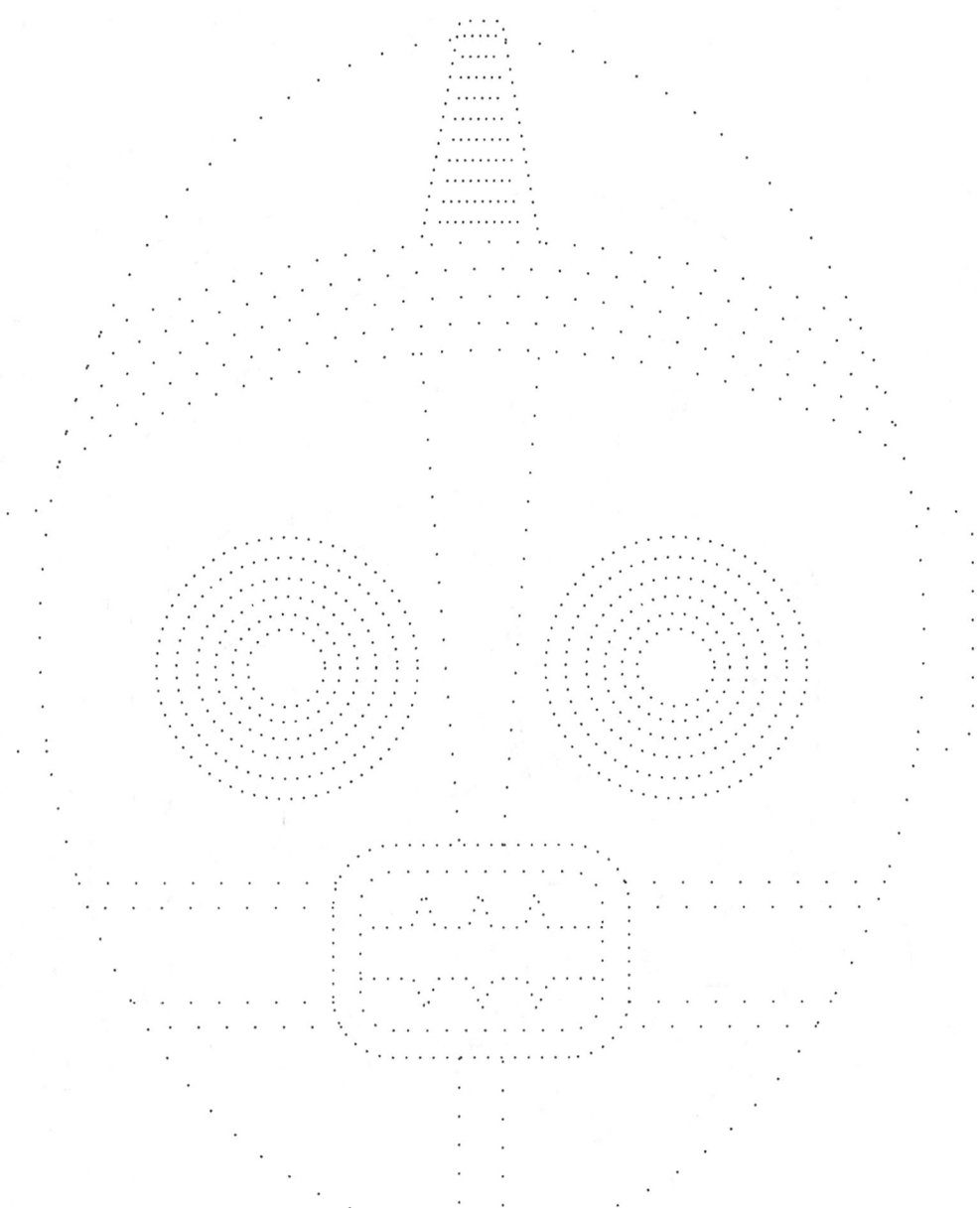

Cheoyongmu Mask

Korea

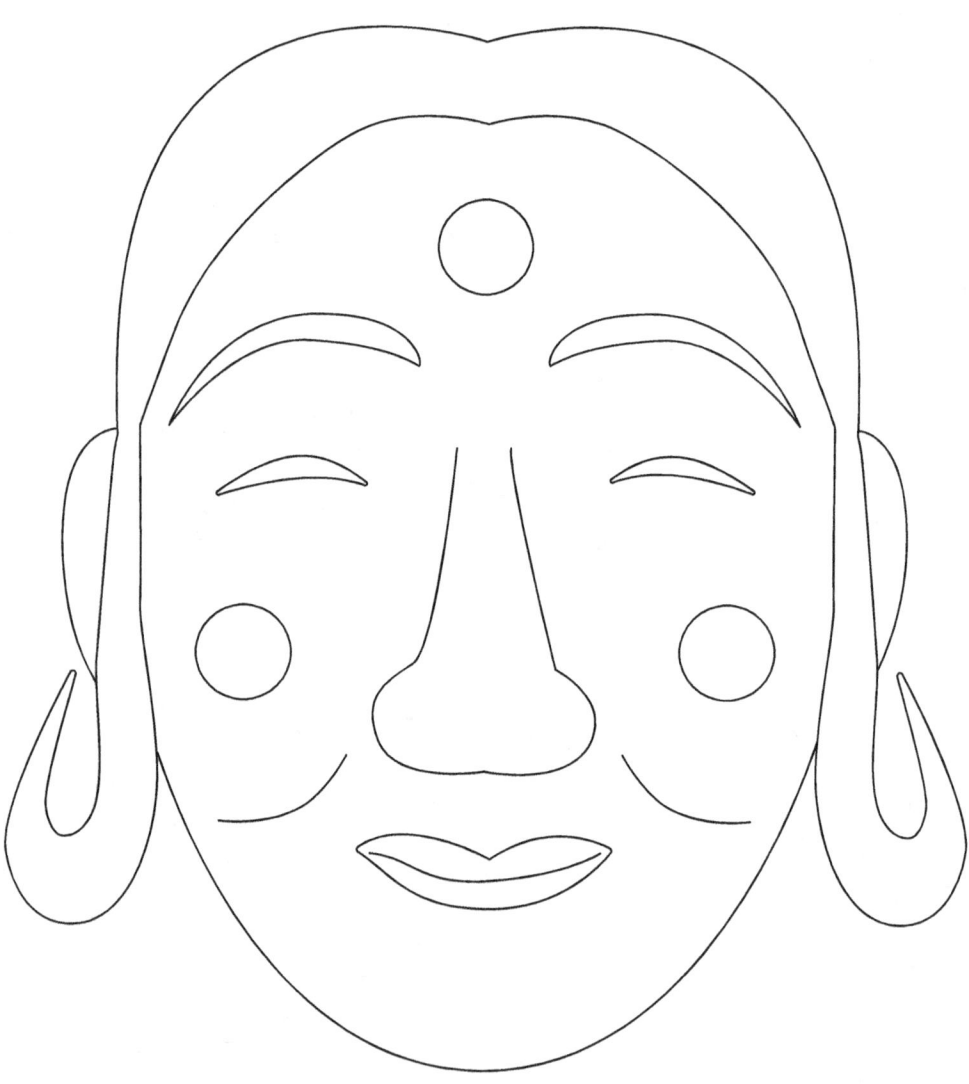

Dancing Devil Mask

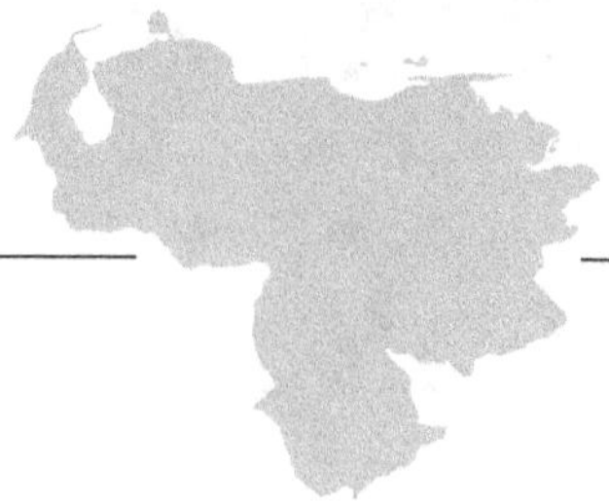

Venezuela

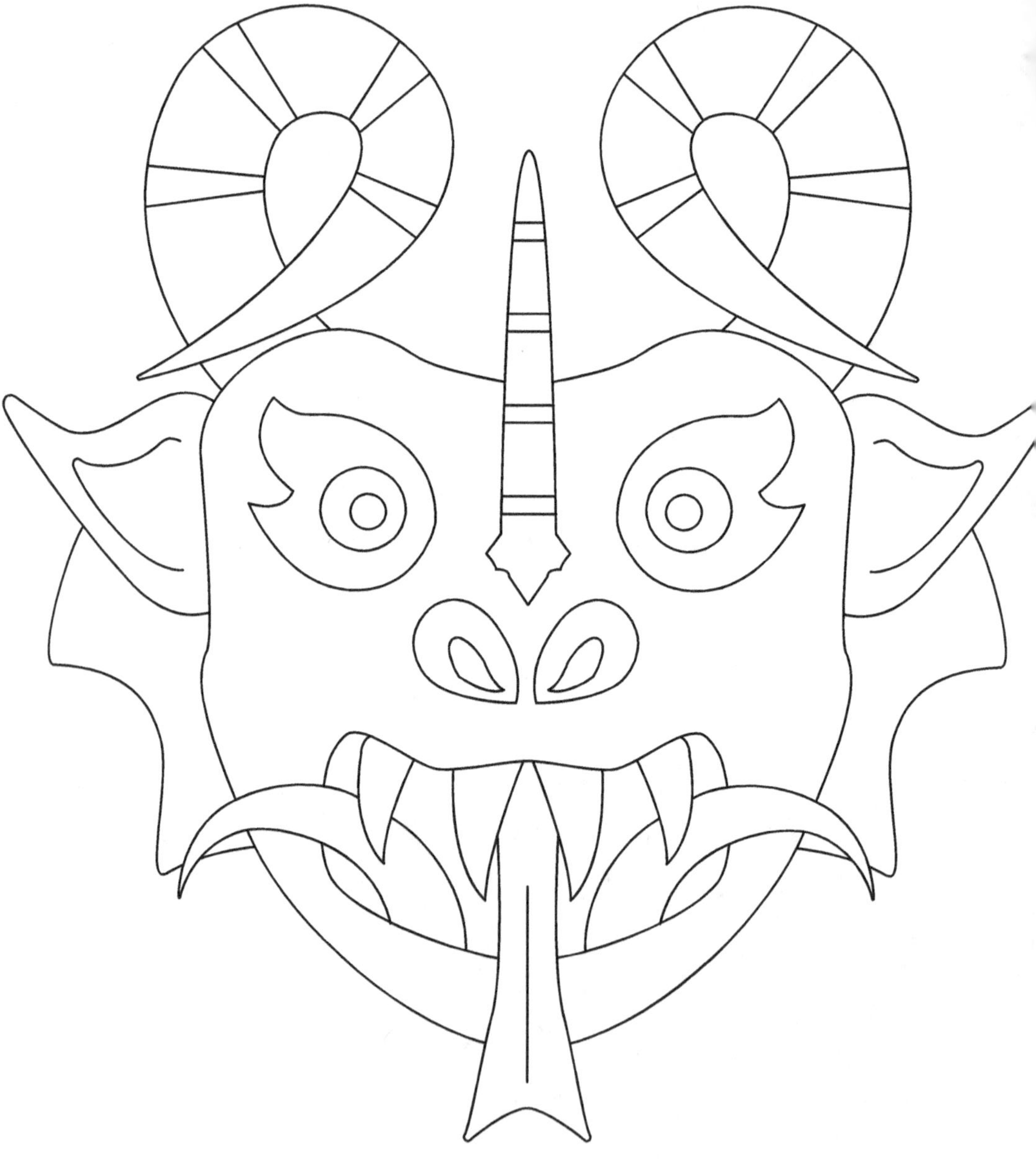

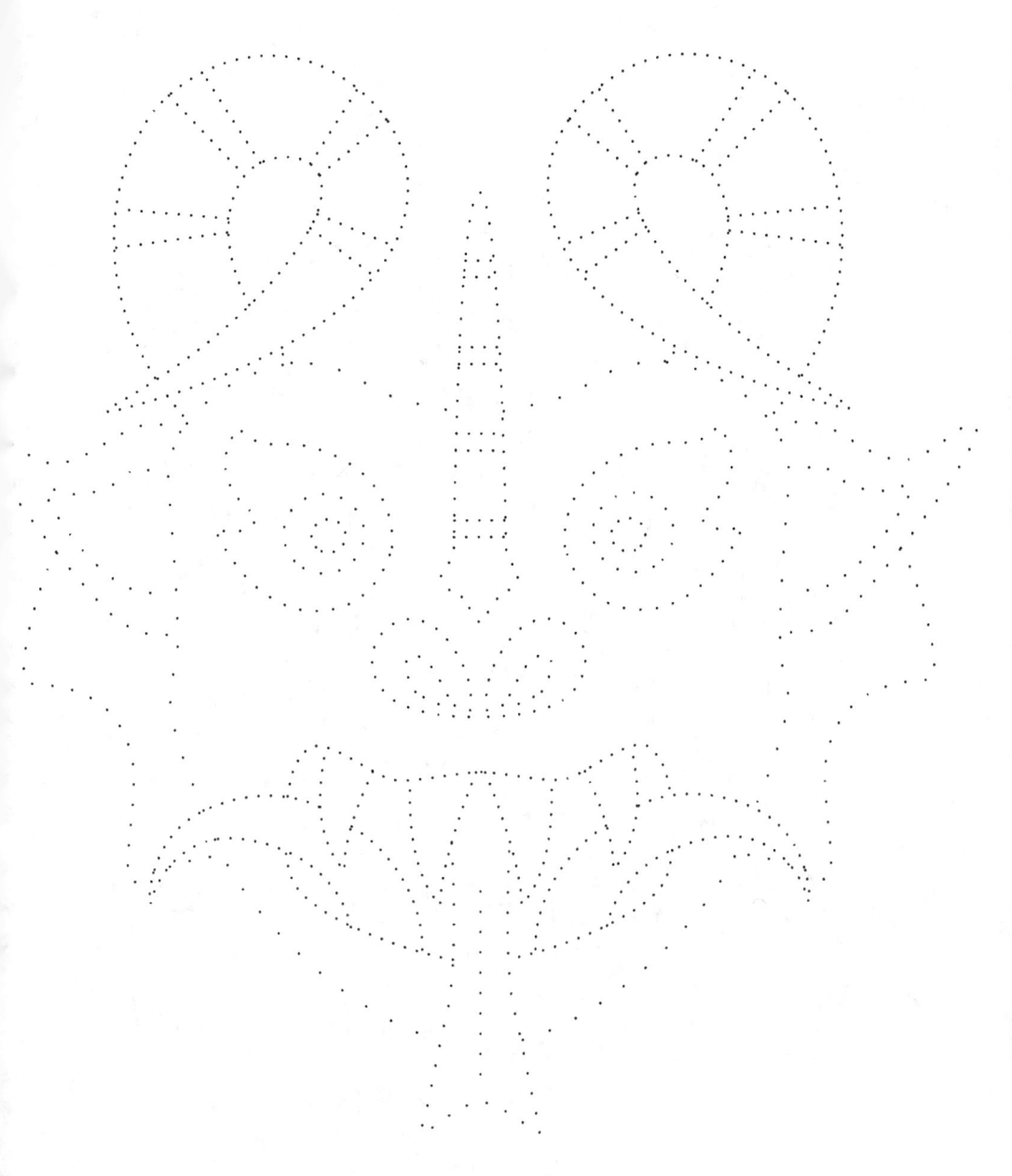

Dayak Mask

Borneo

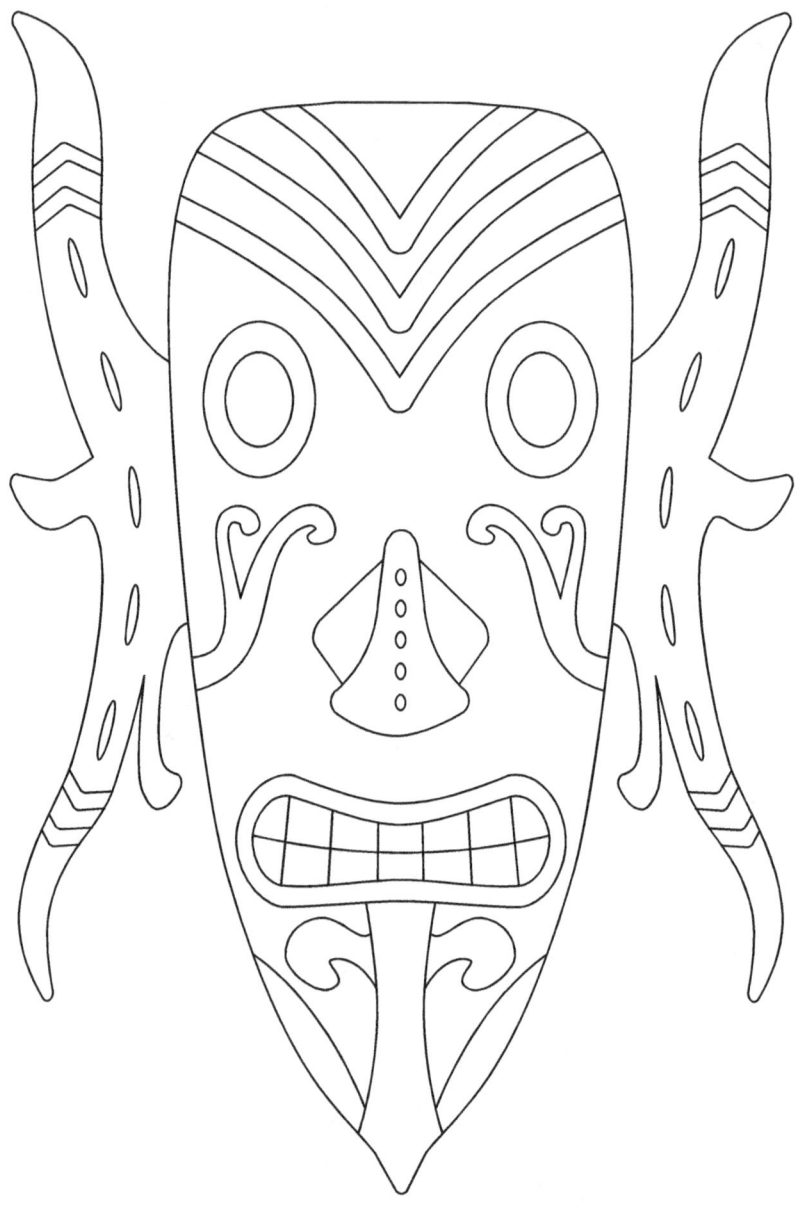

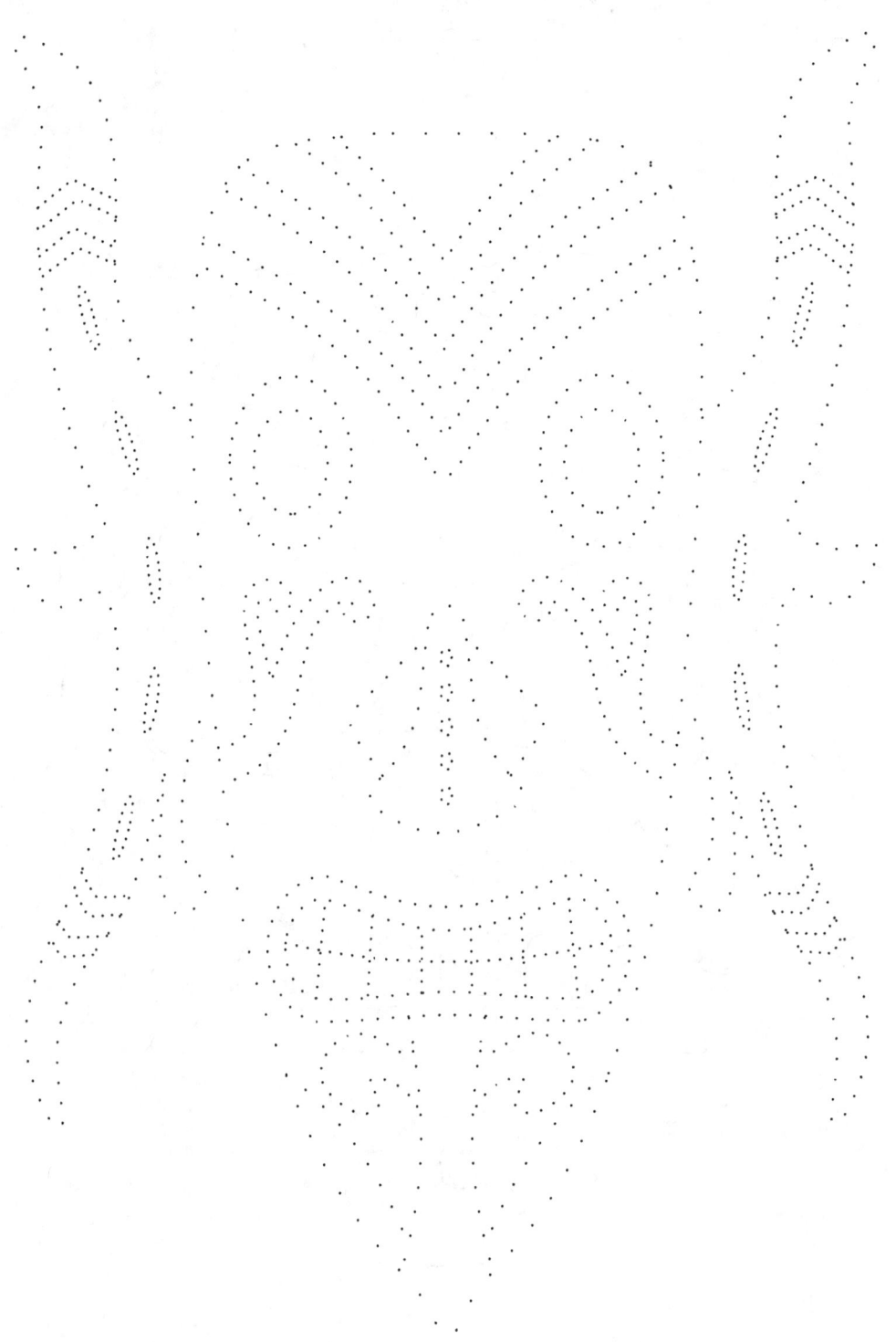

Day of the Dead Mask

Mexico

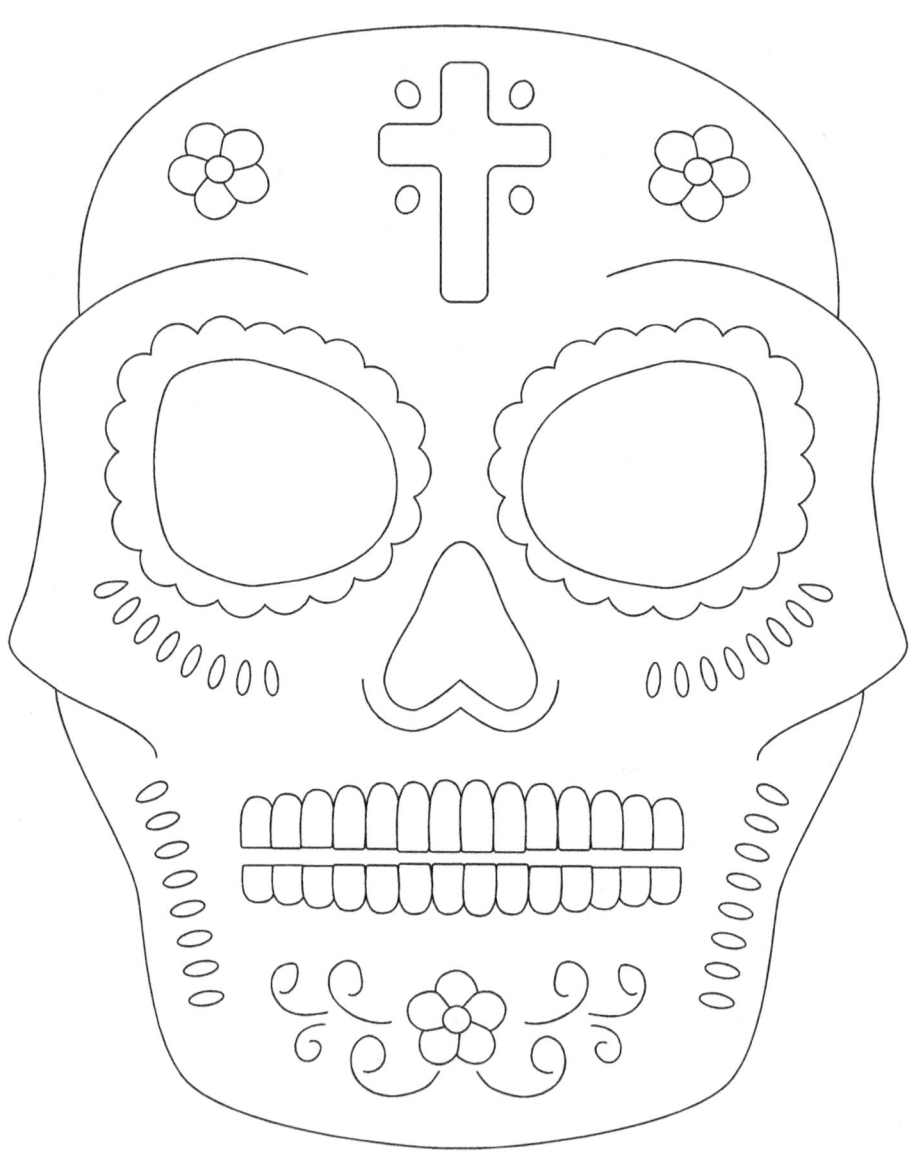

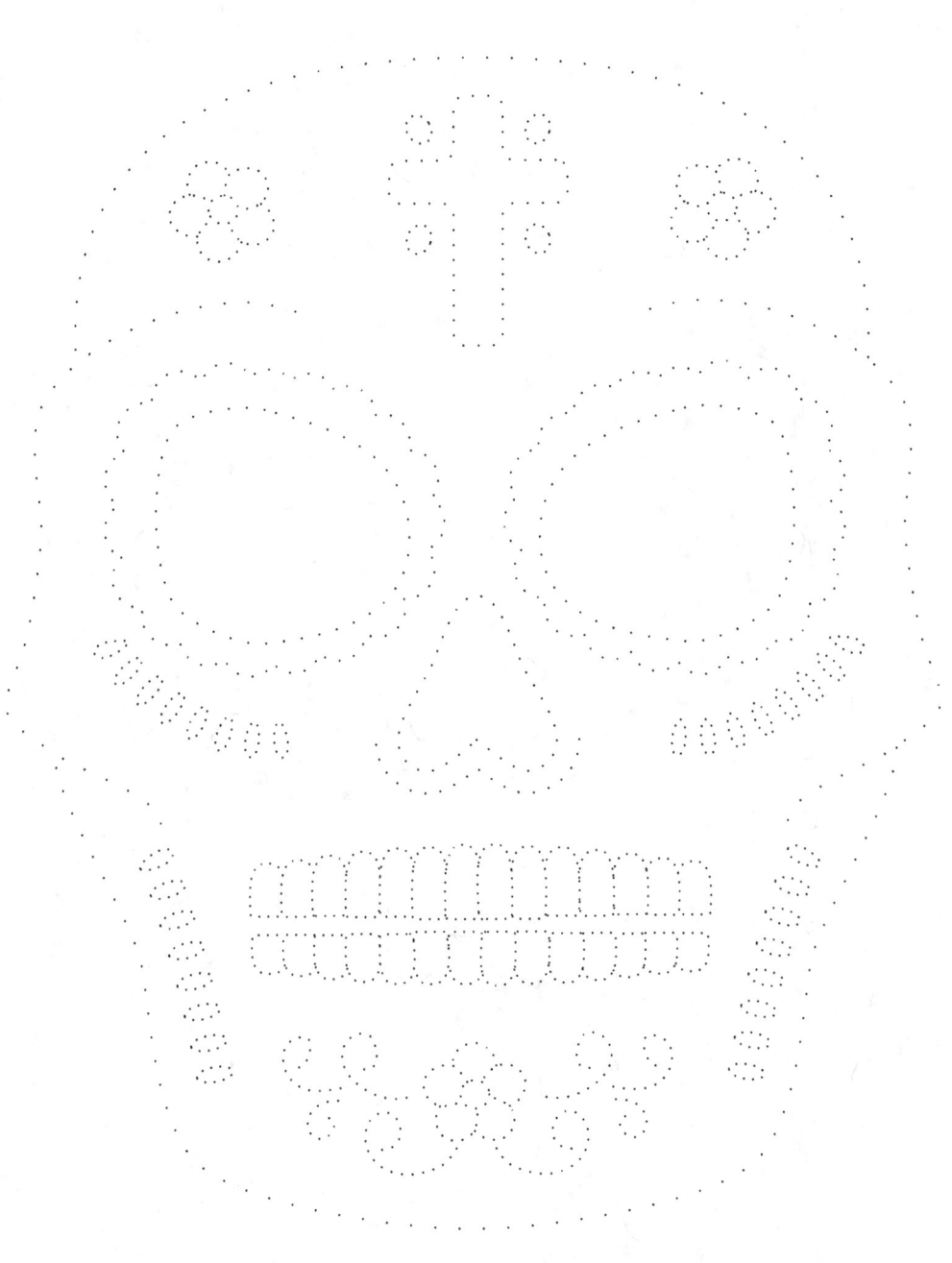

Dionysus Mask

Greece

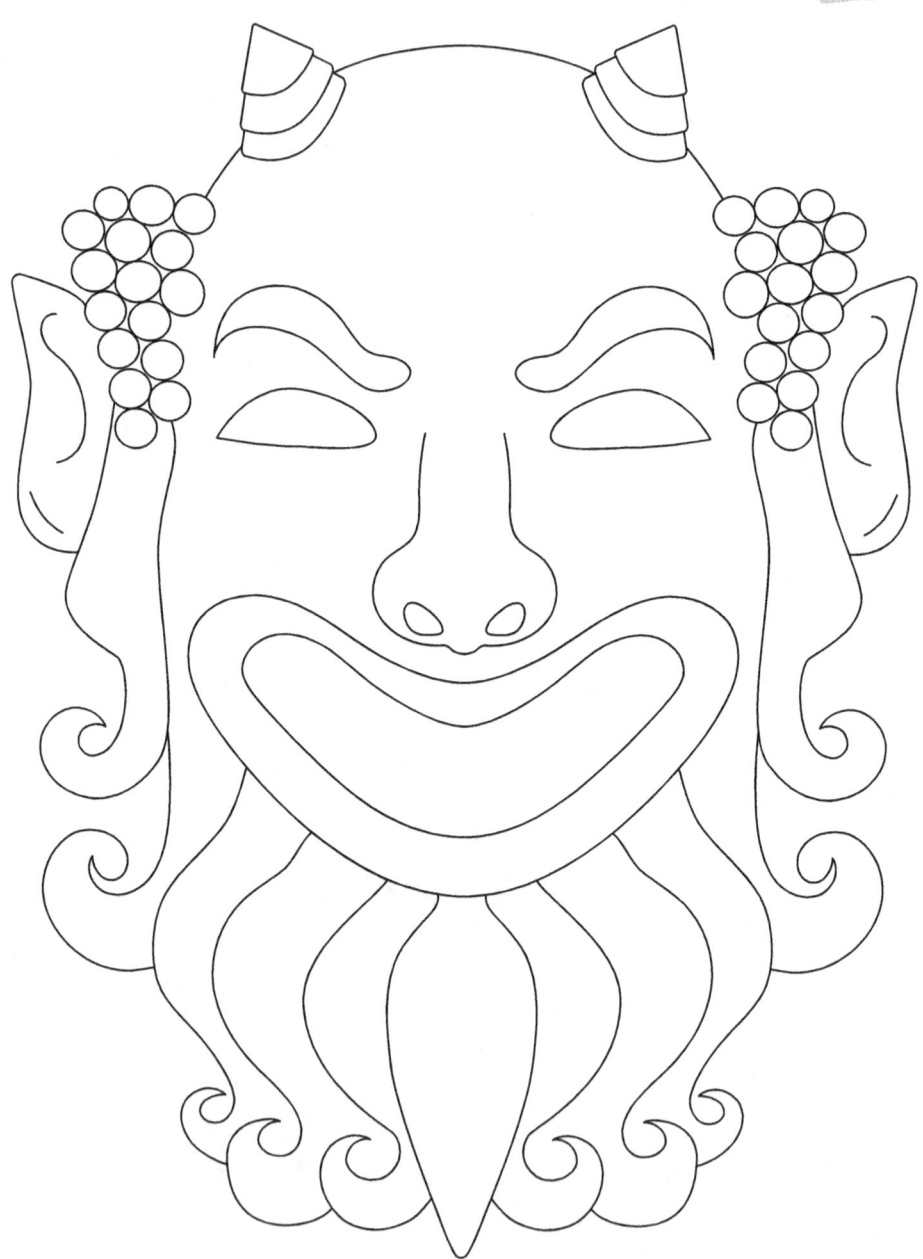

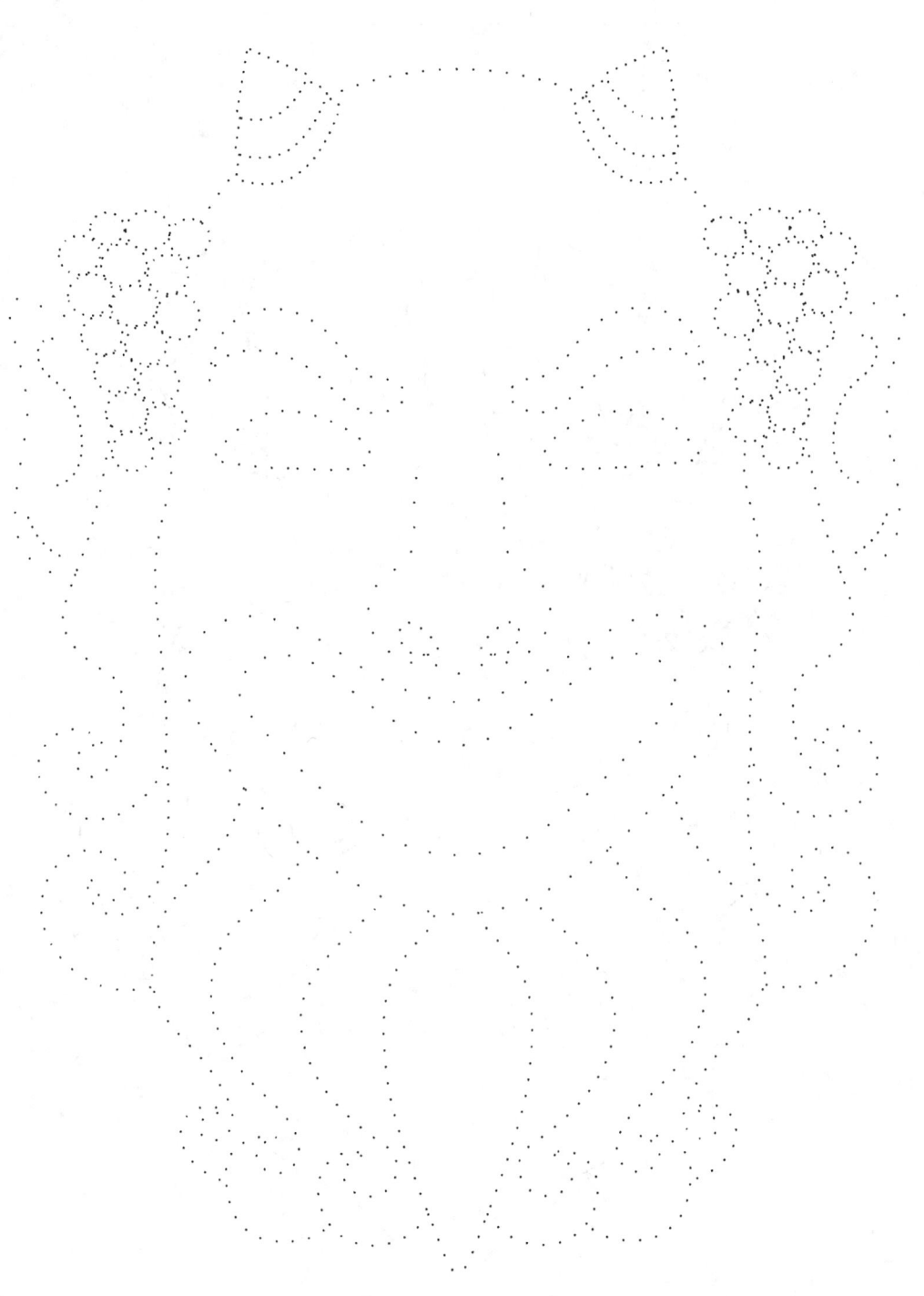

Garuda Mask
India

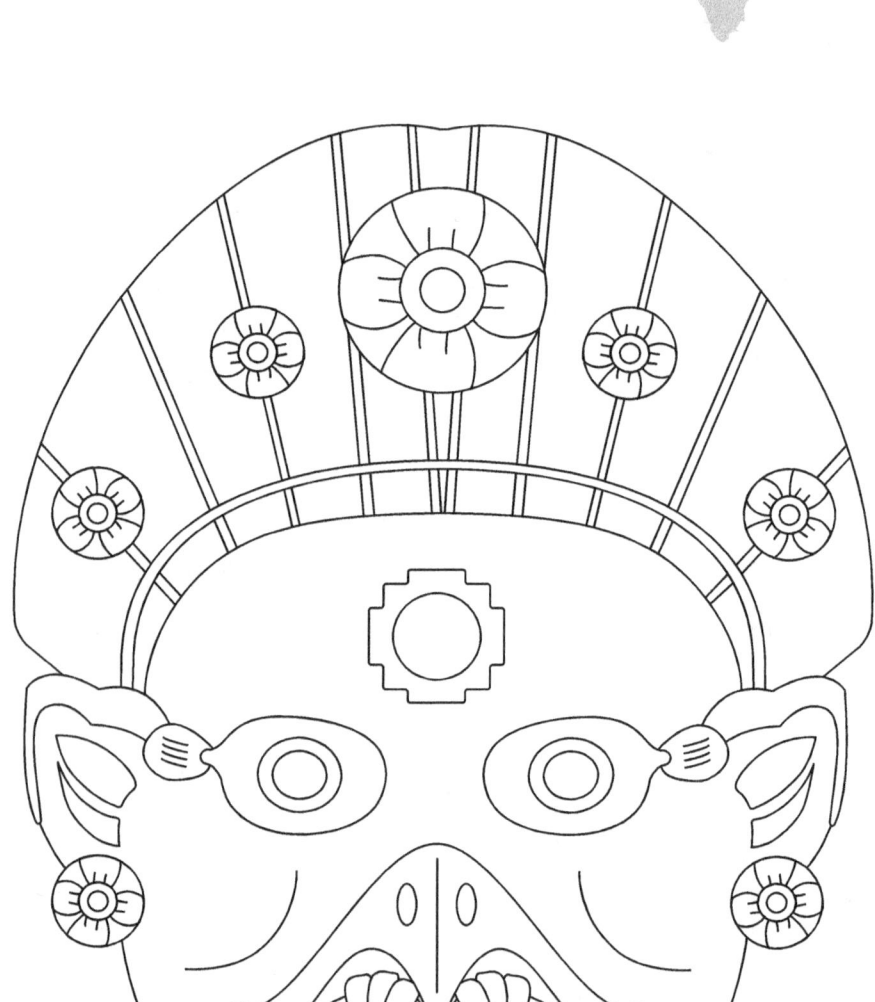

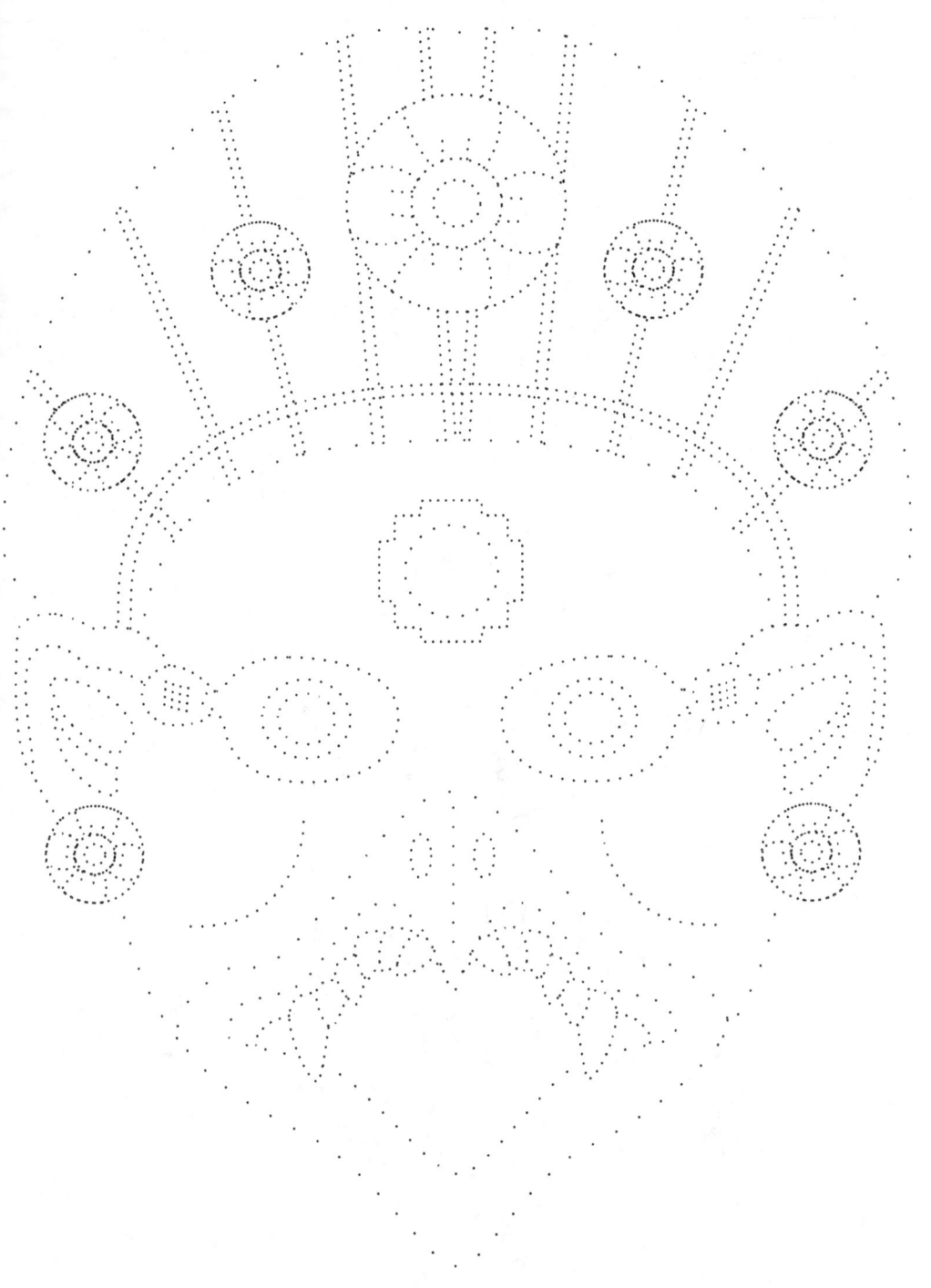

Guro Antelope Mask

Ivory Coast

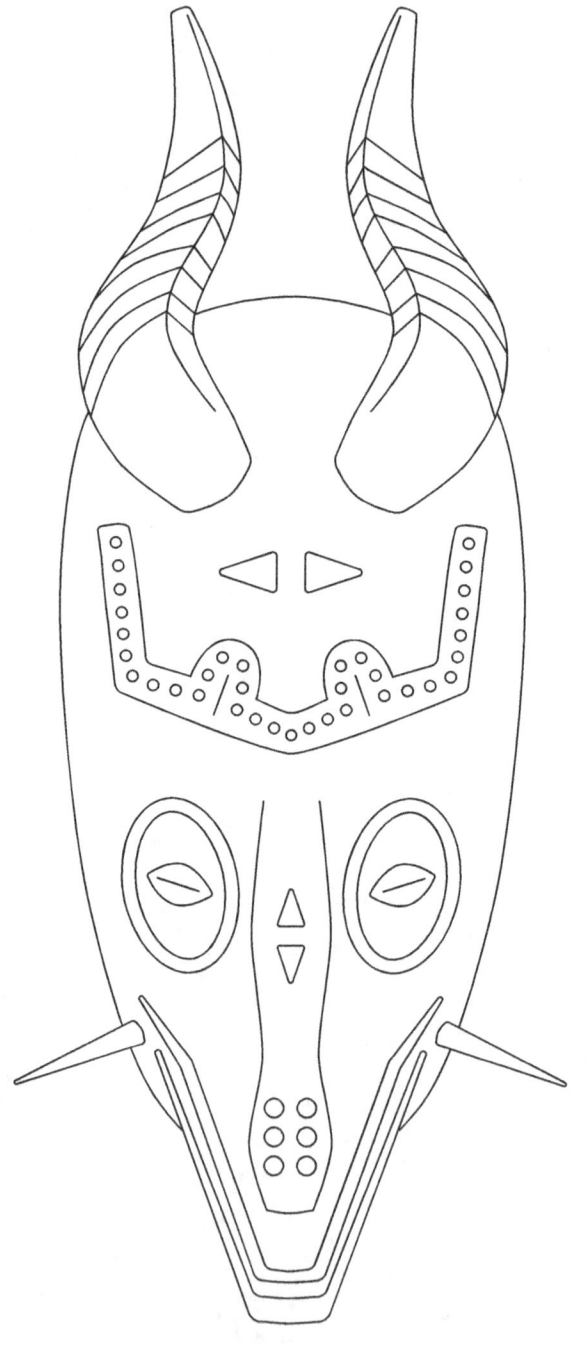

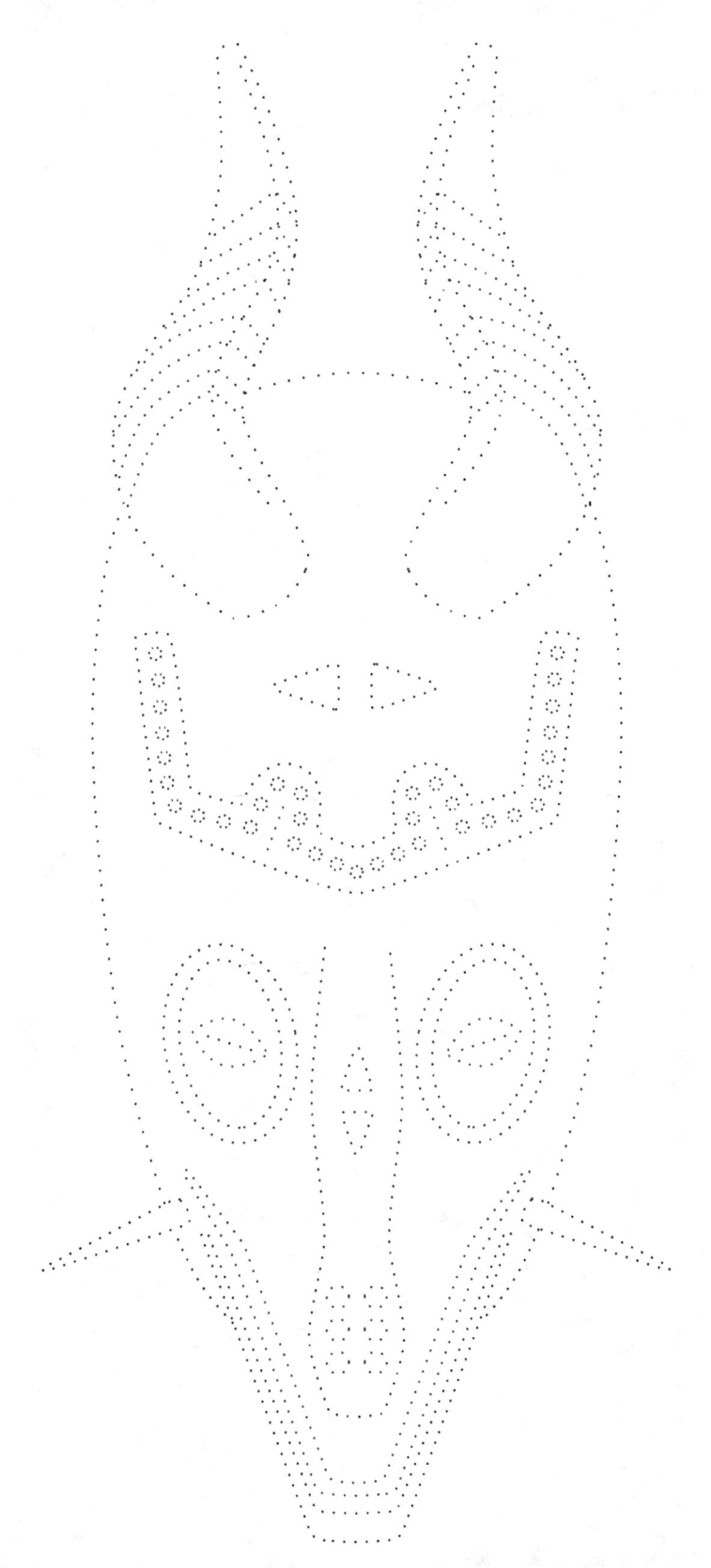

Hannya Mask

Japan

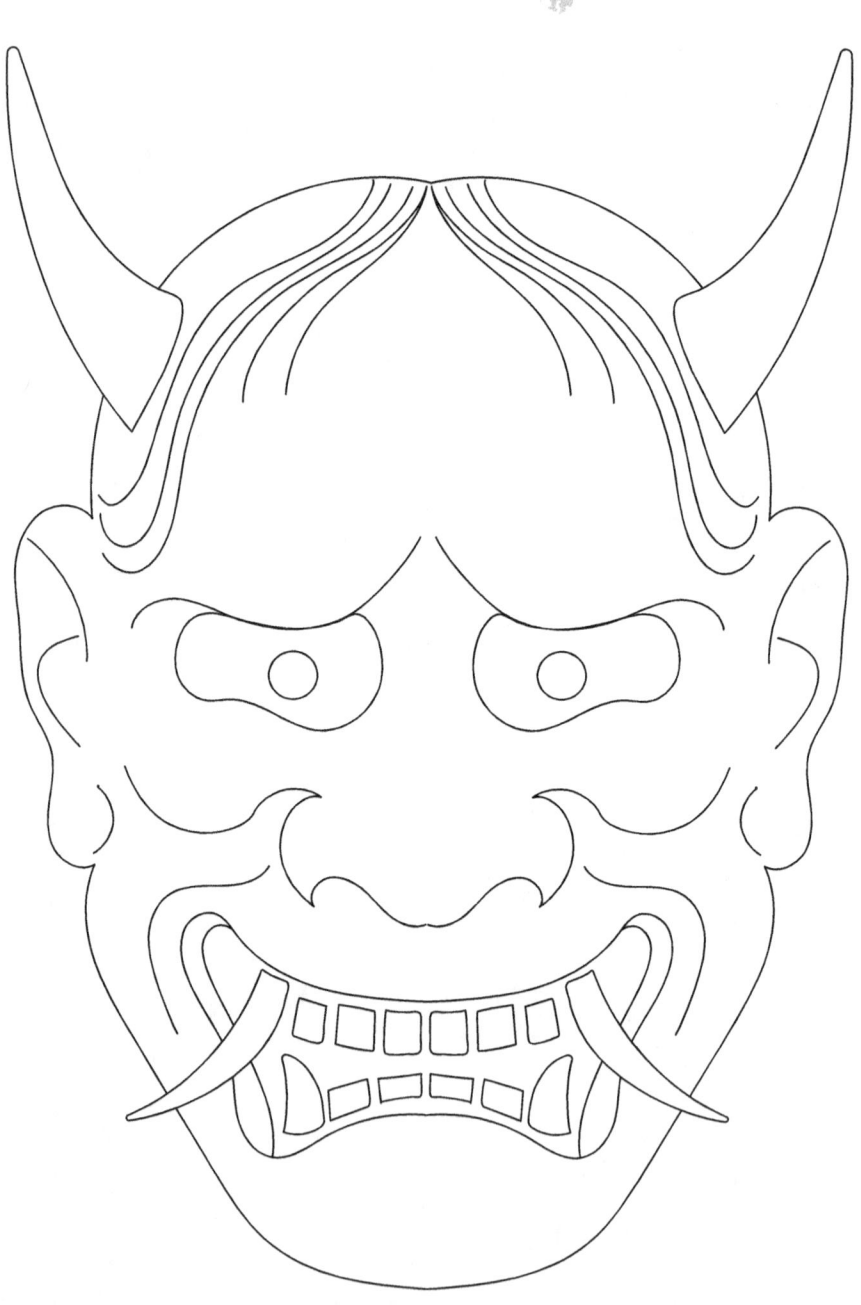

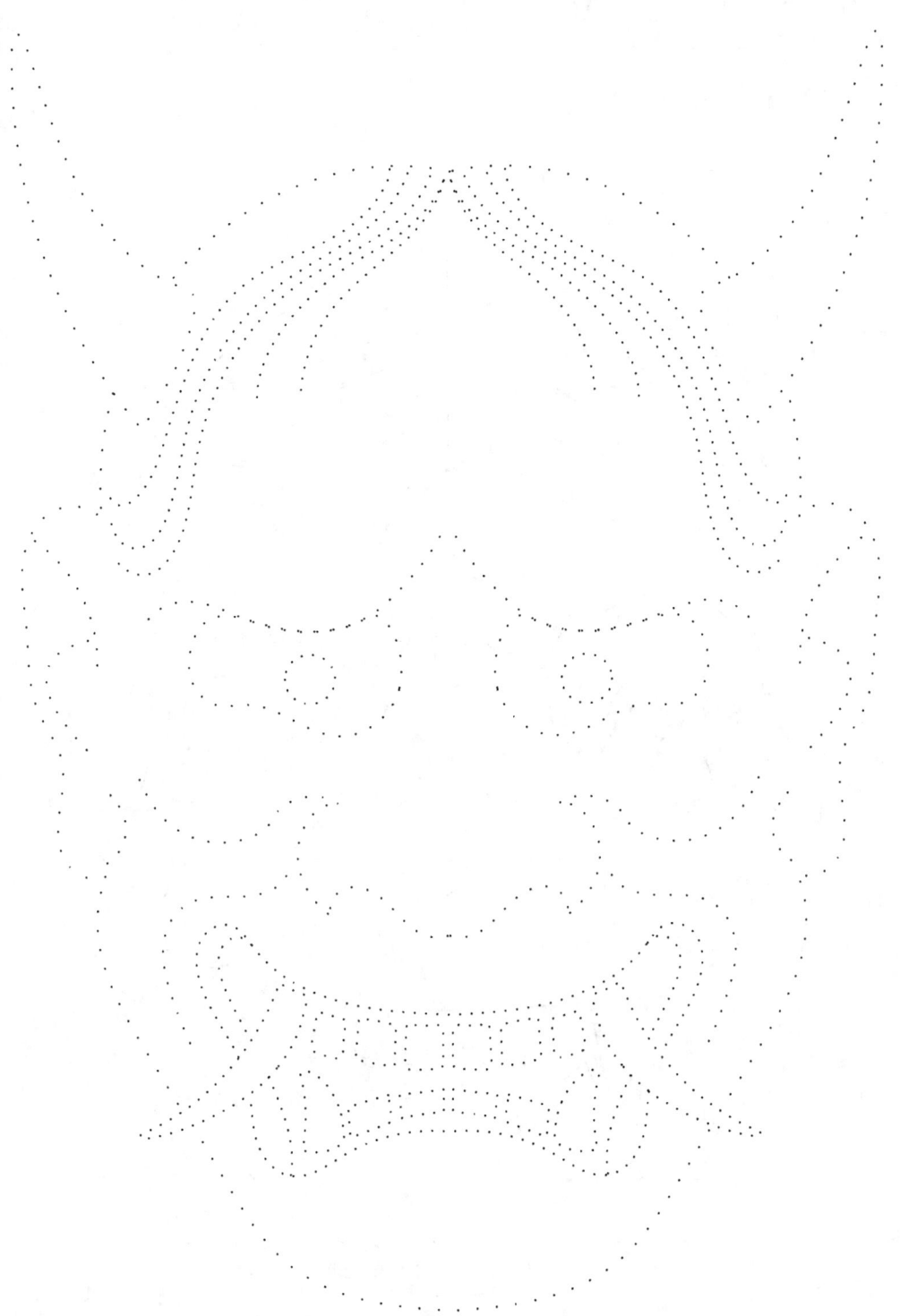

Hanuman Mask

Java, Indonesia

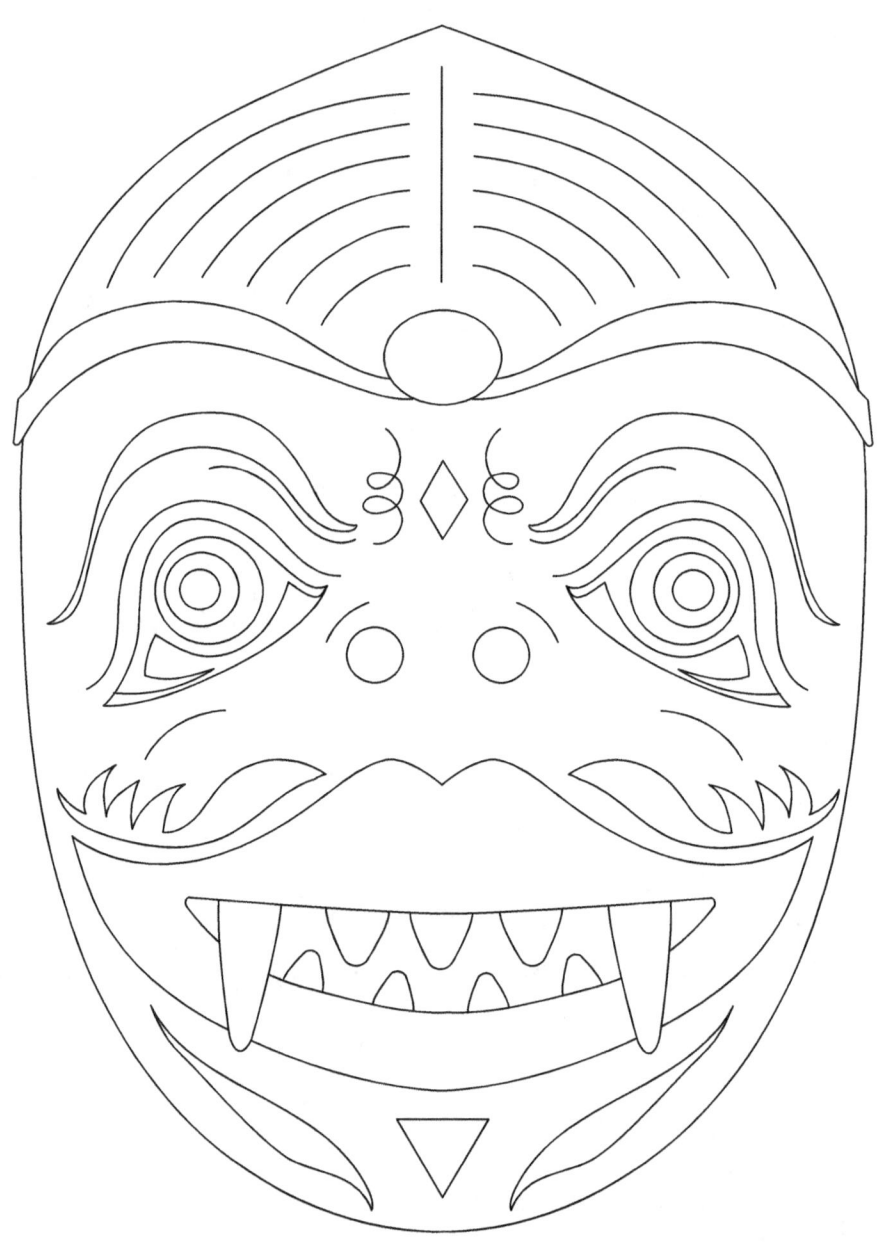

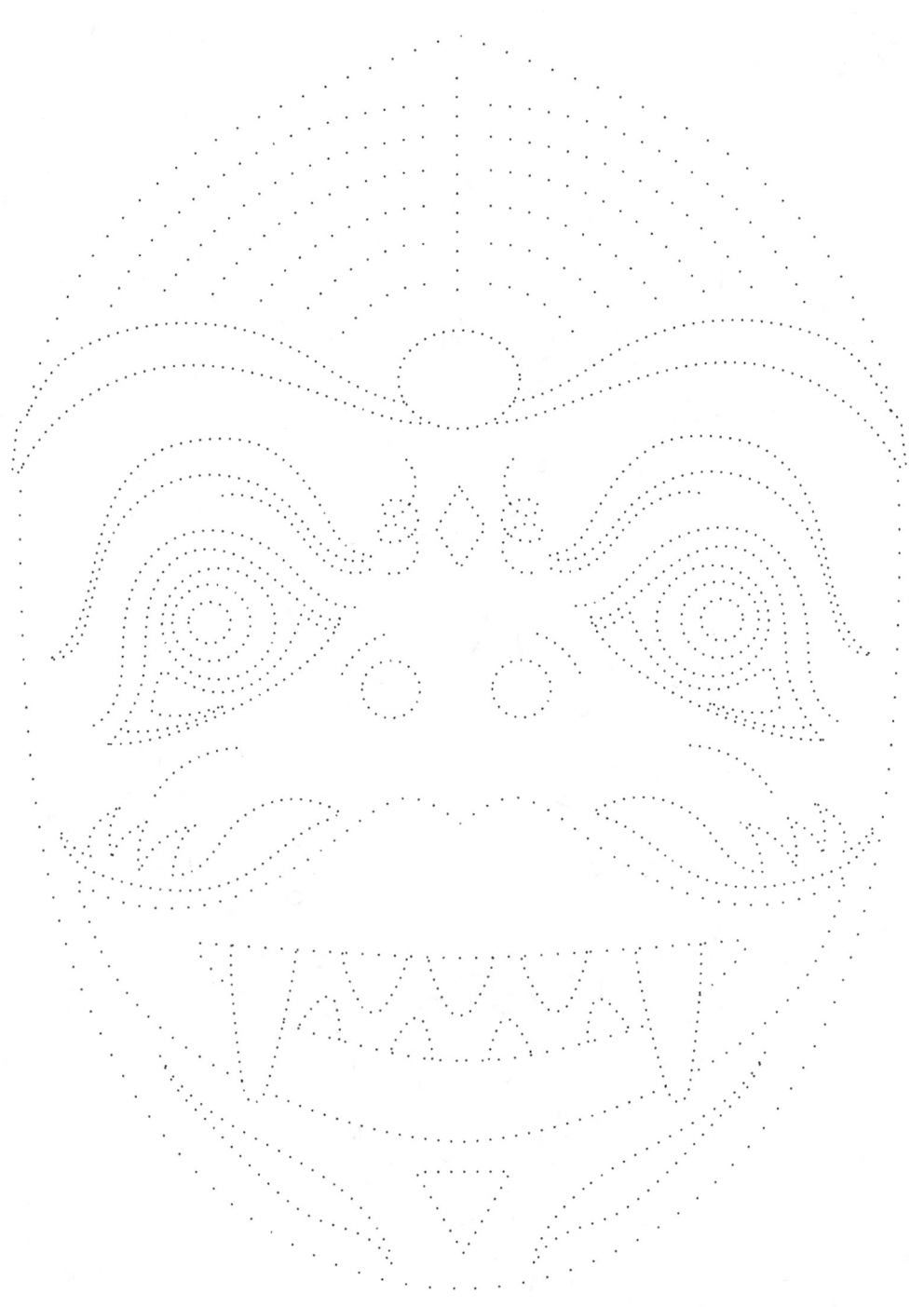

Kali Mask
India

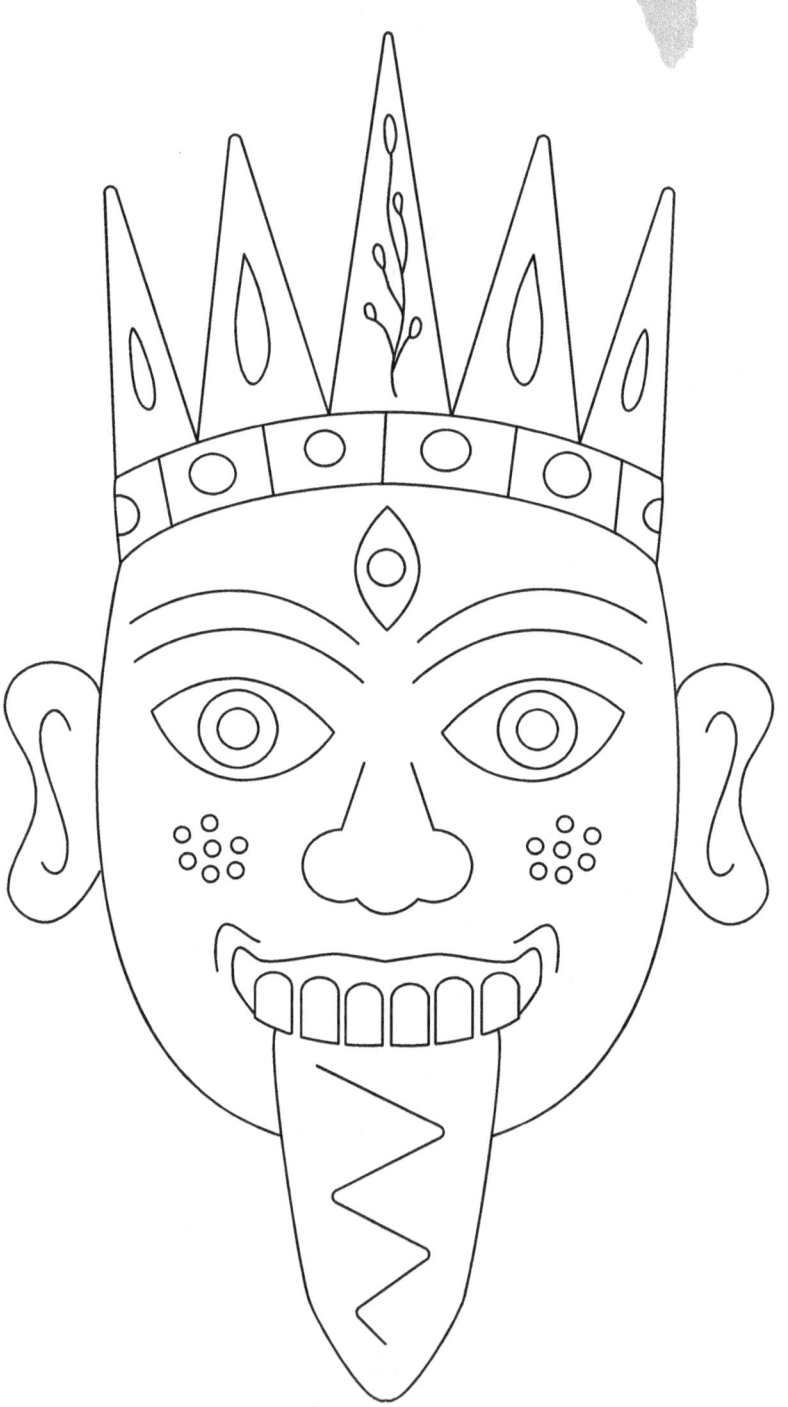

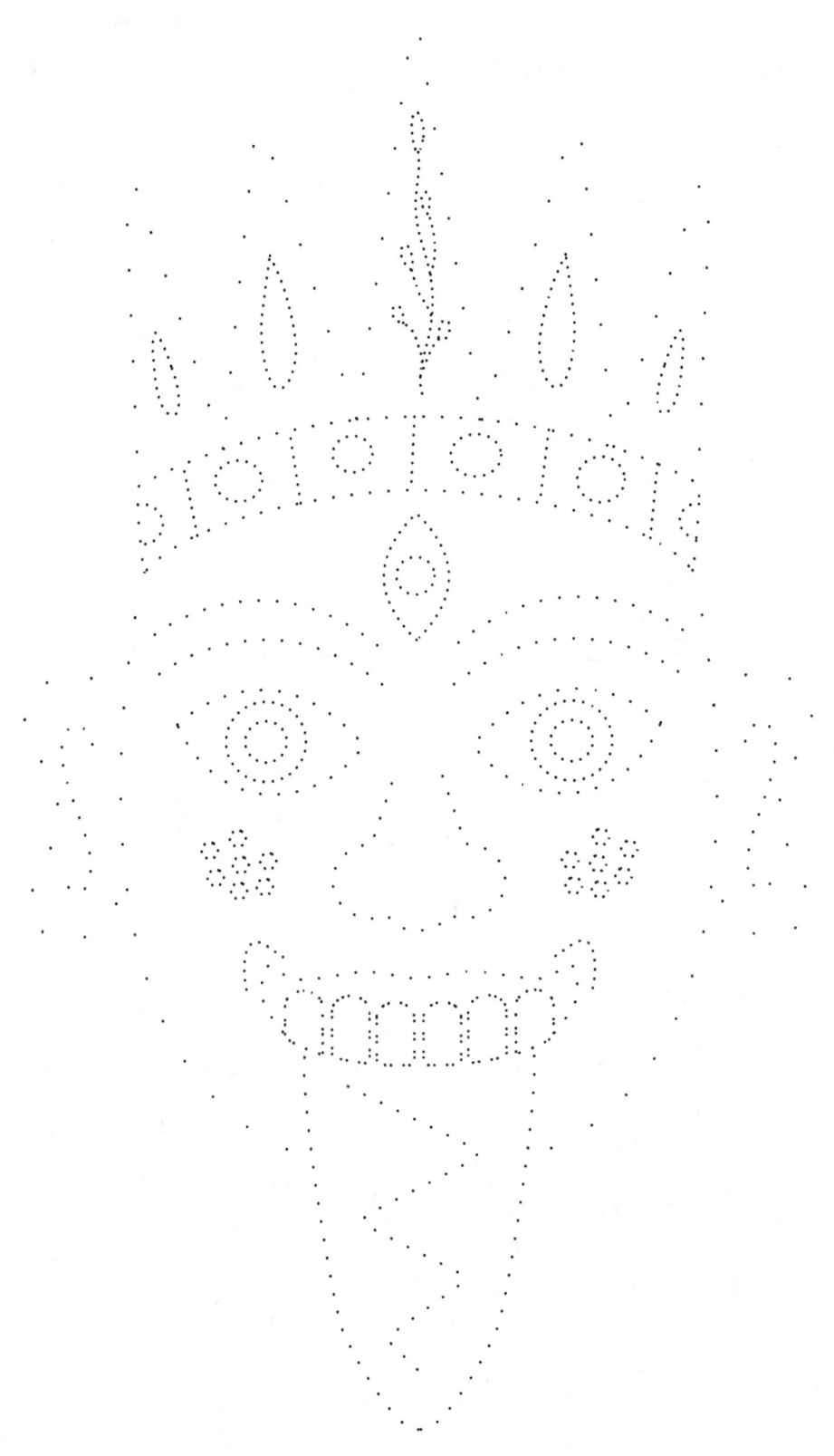

Kamayura Mask

Brazil

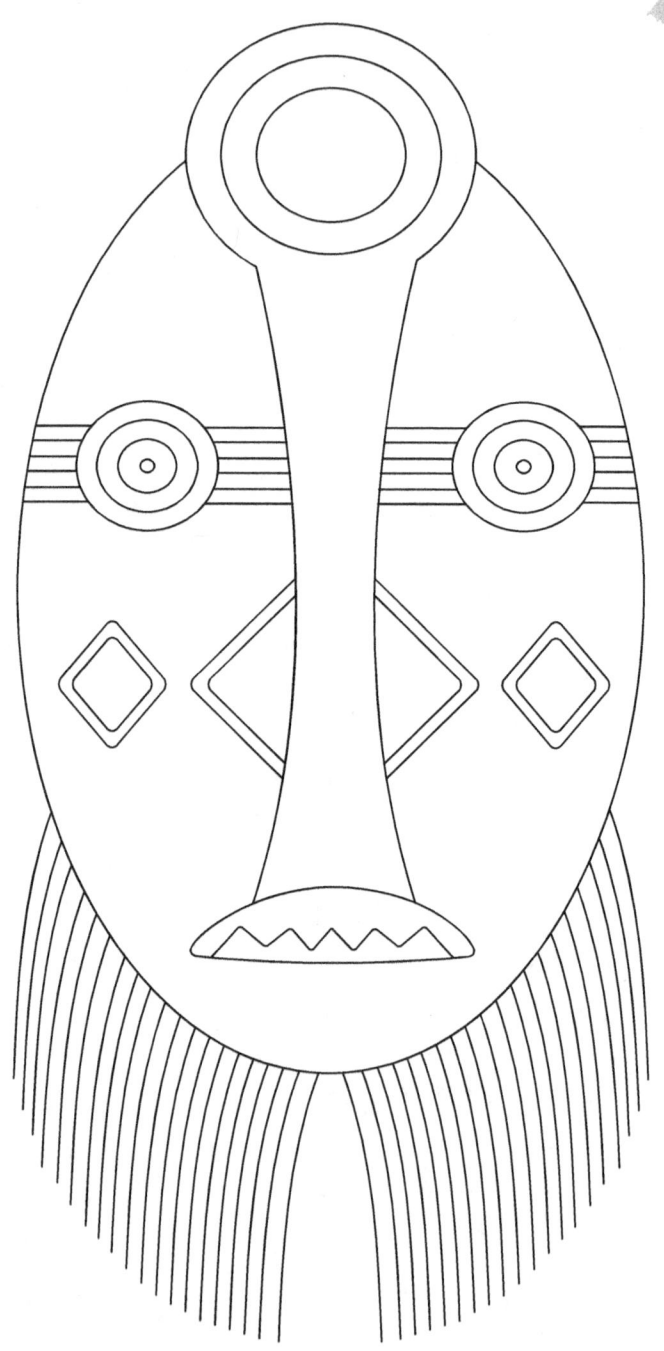

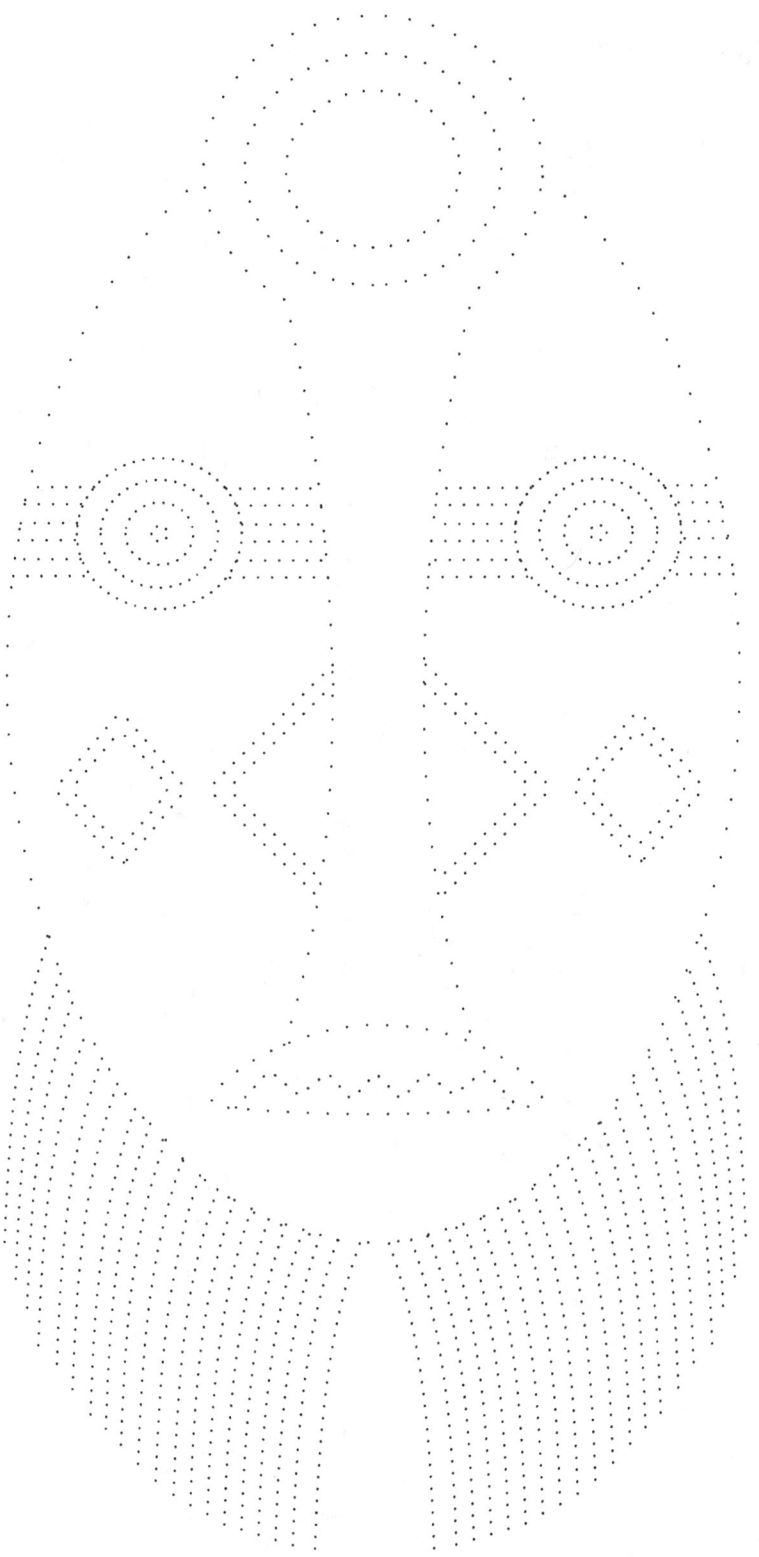

Maori Mask

New Zealand

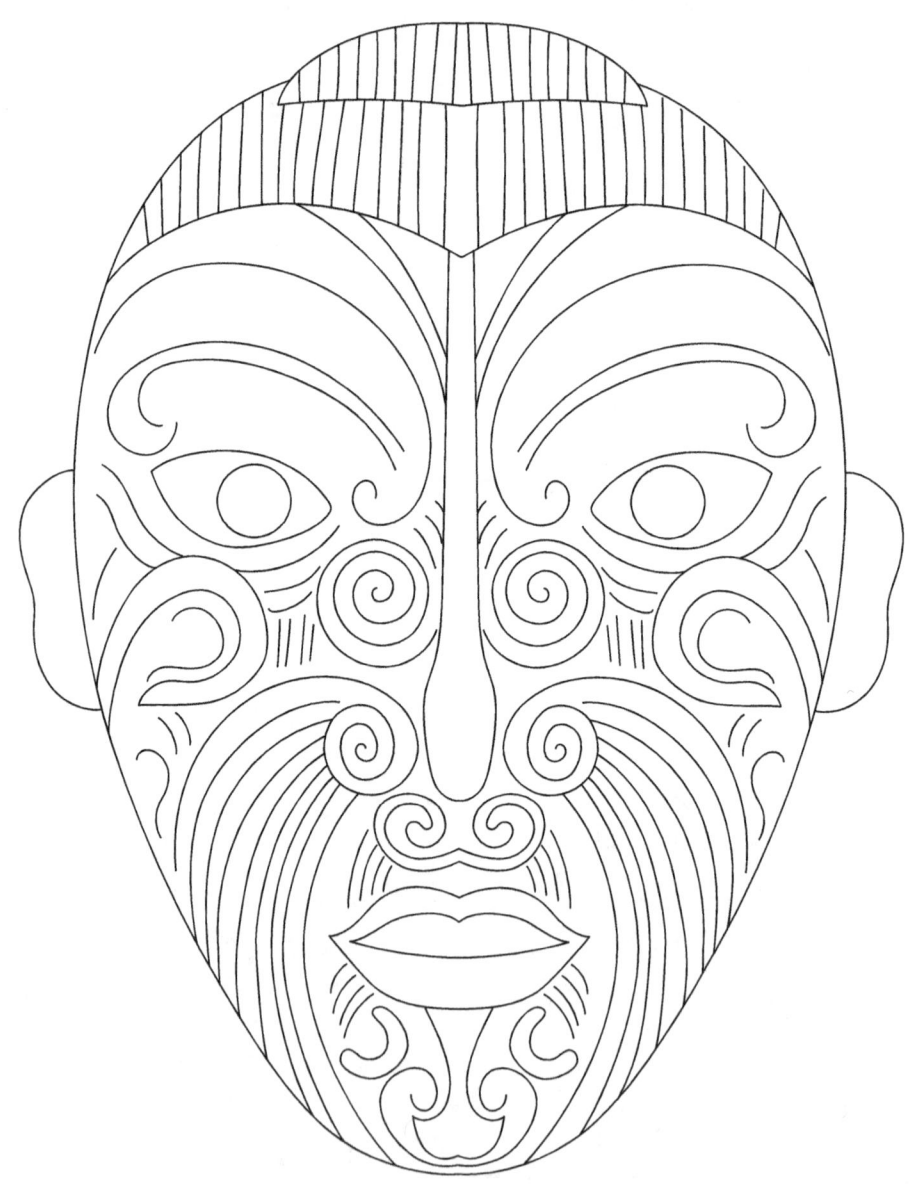

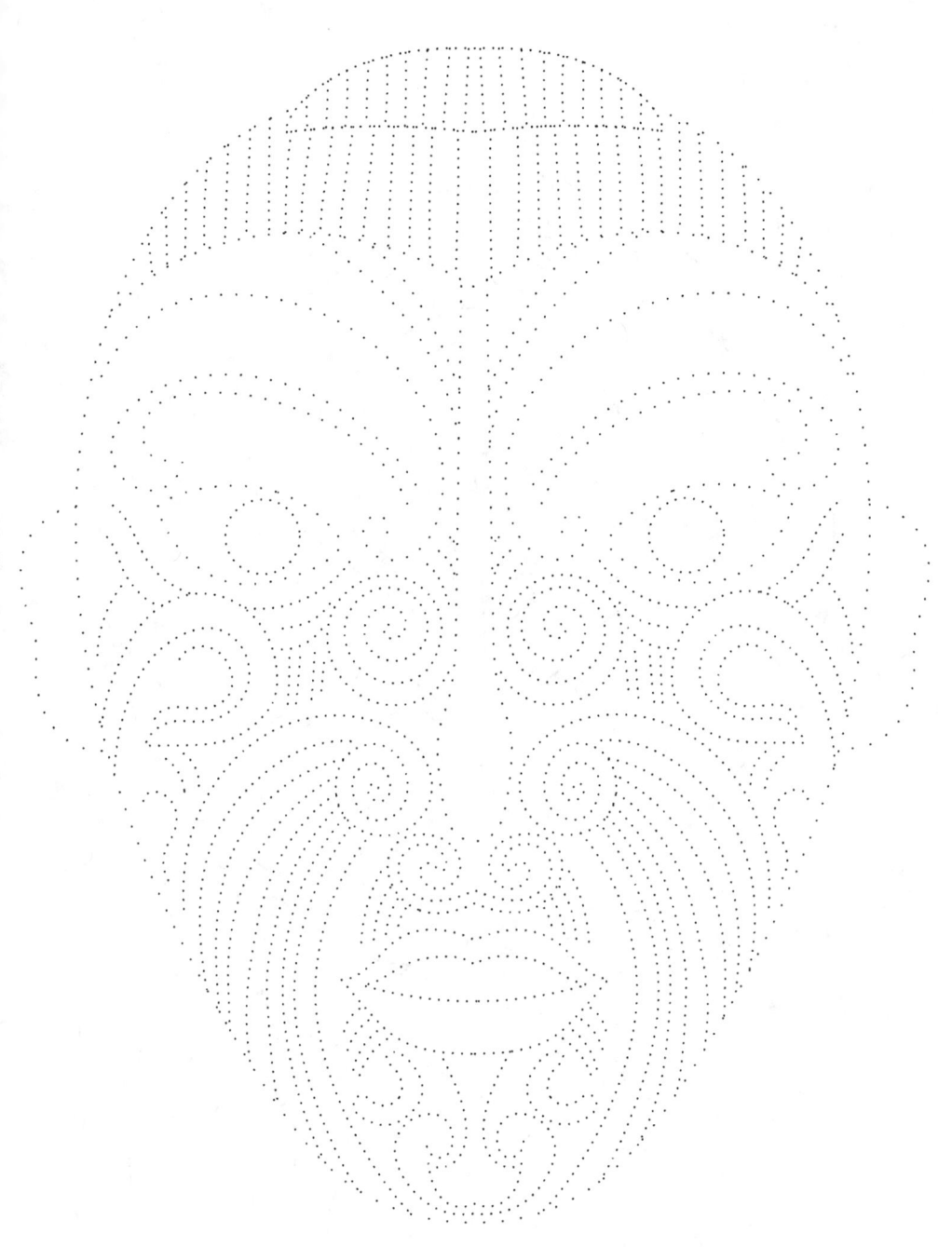

Mikishi Mask

DR Congo

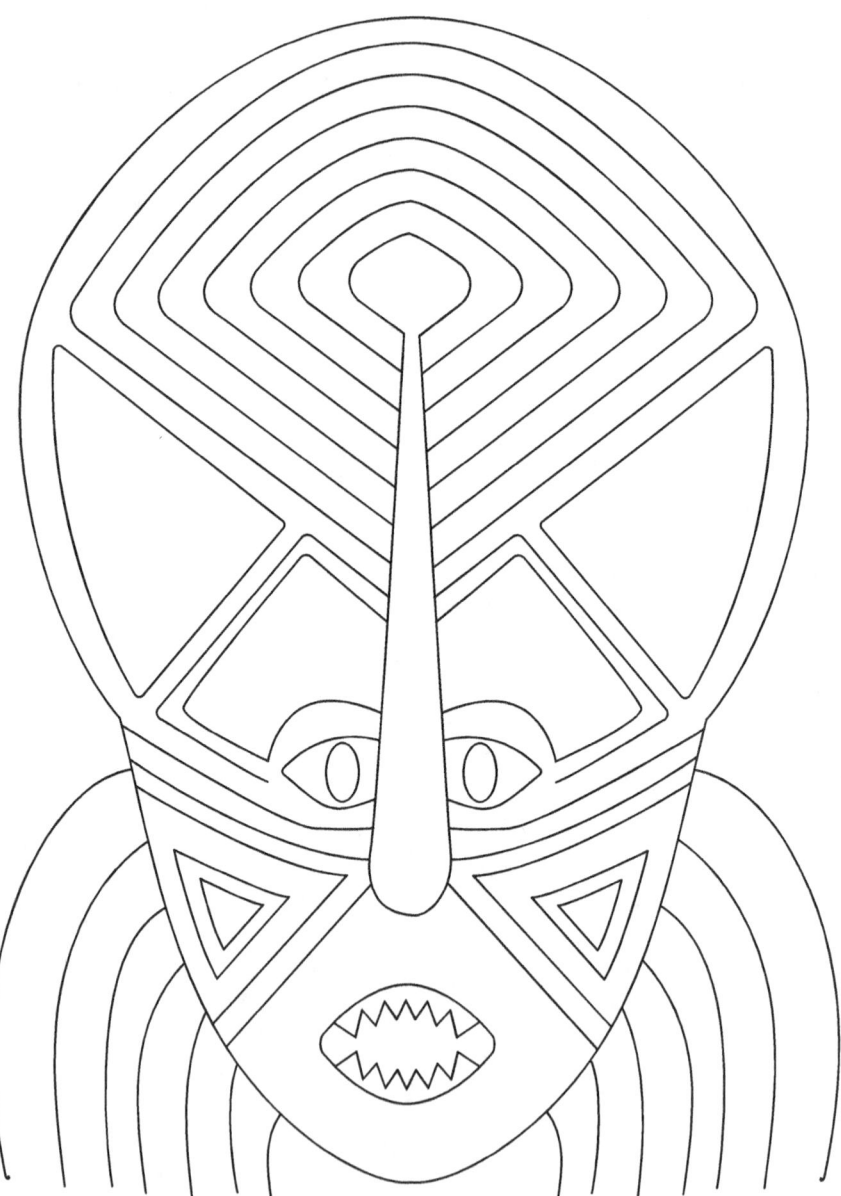

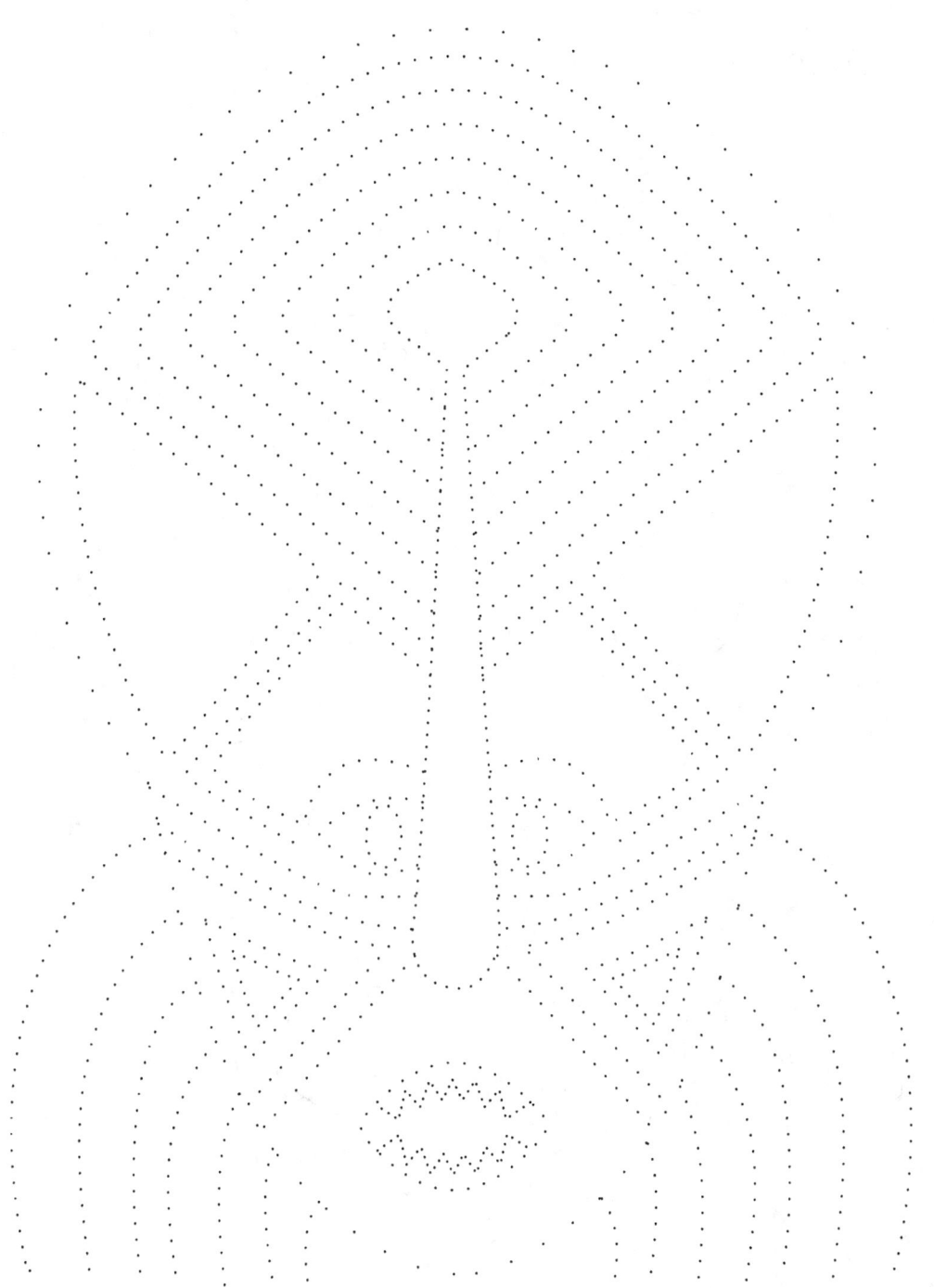

Monkey Mask
Ecuador

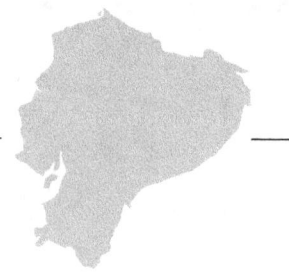

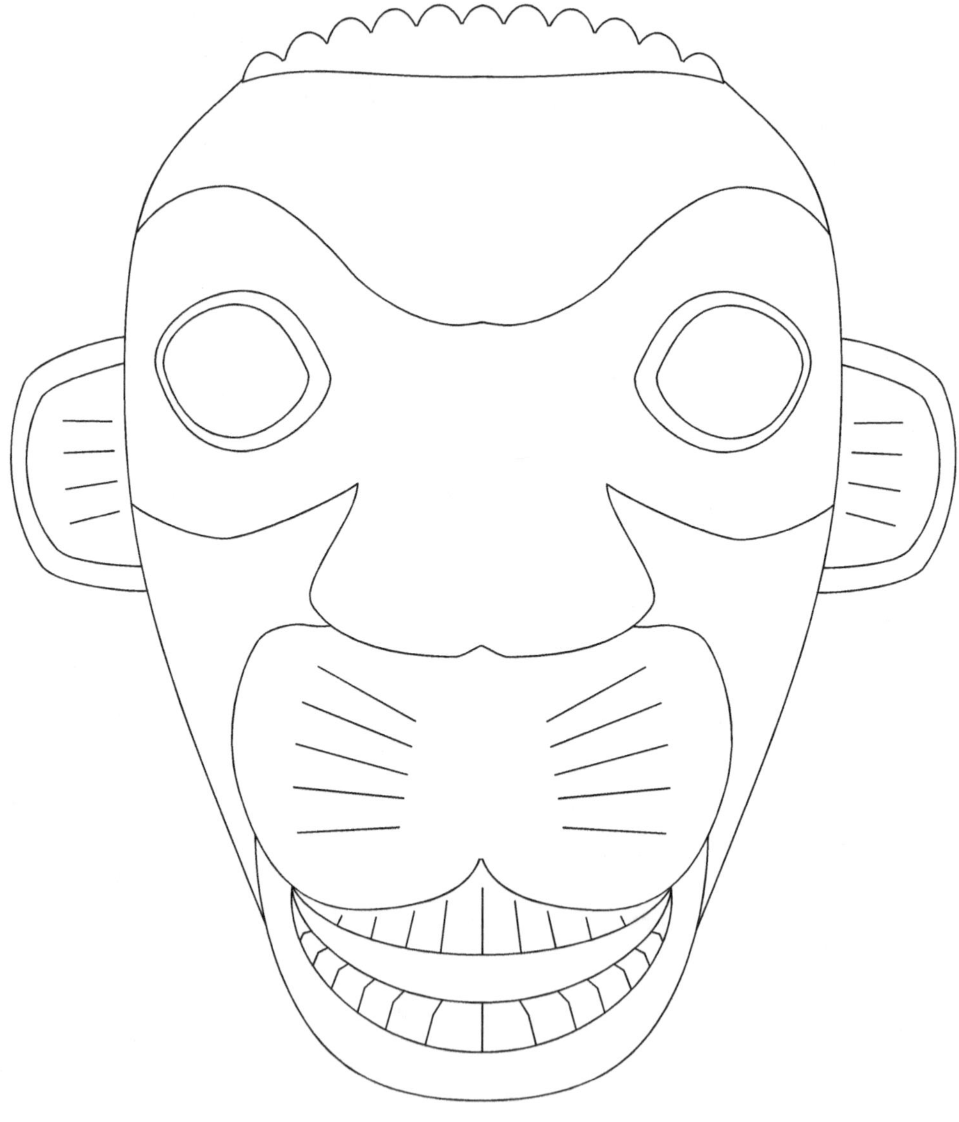

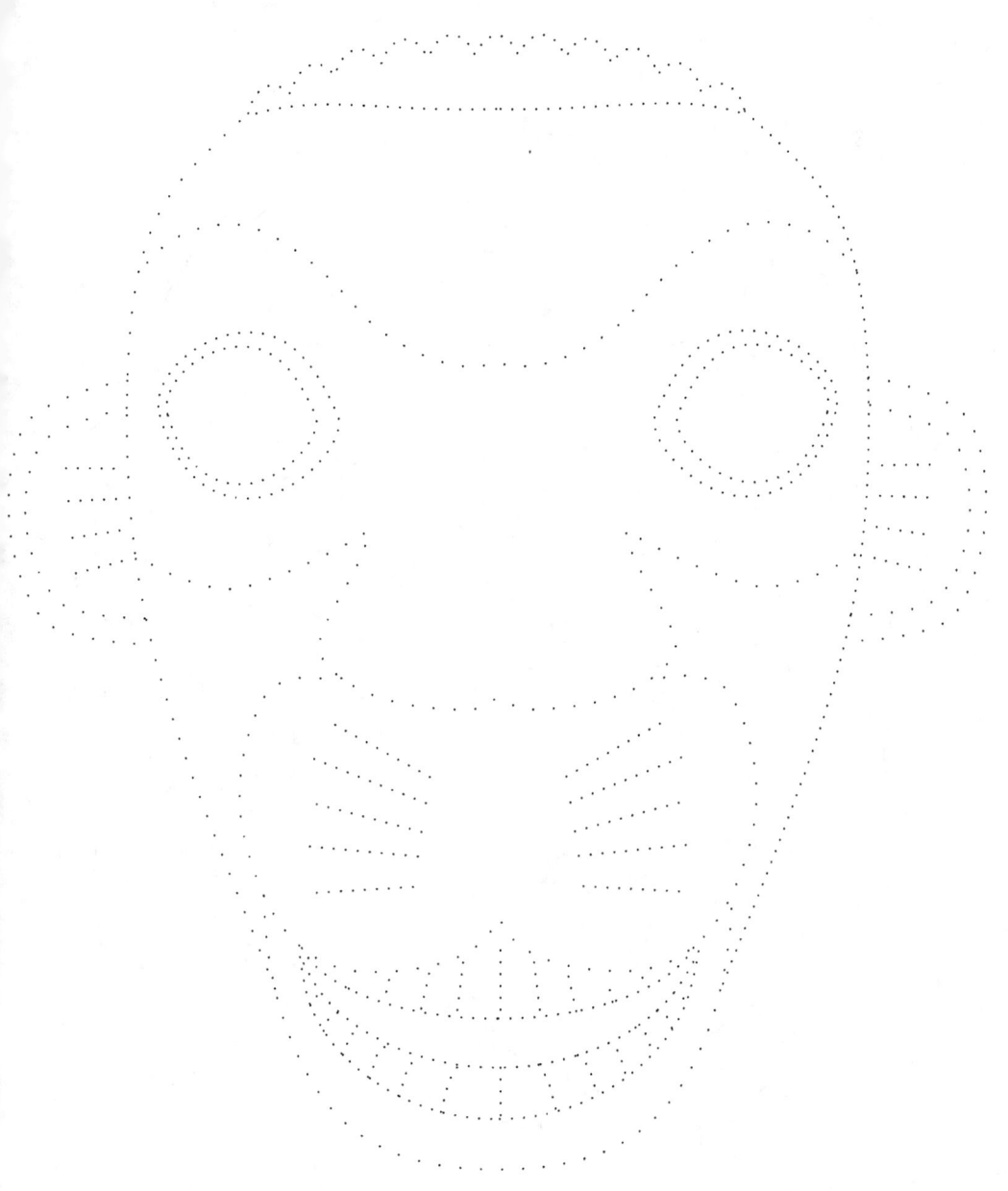

Monkey Mask

Japan

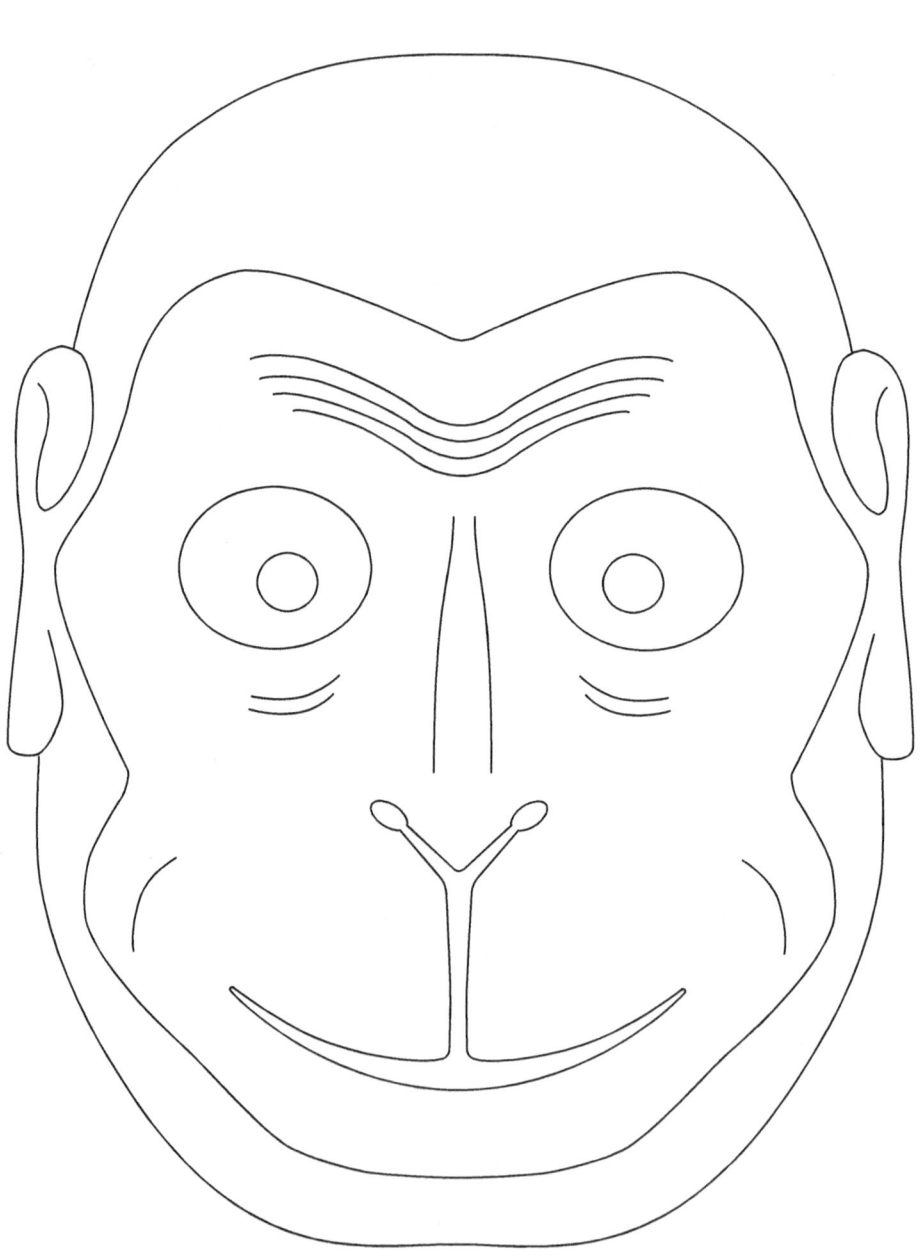

Namahage Mask

Japan

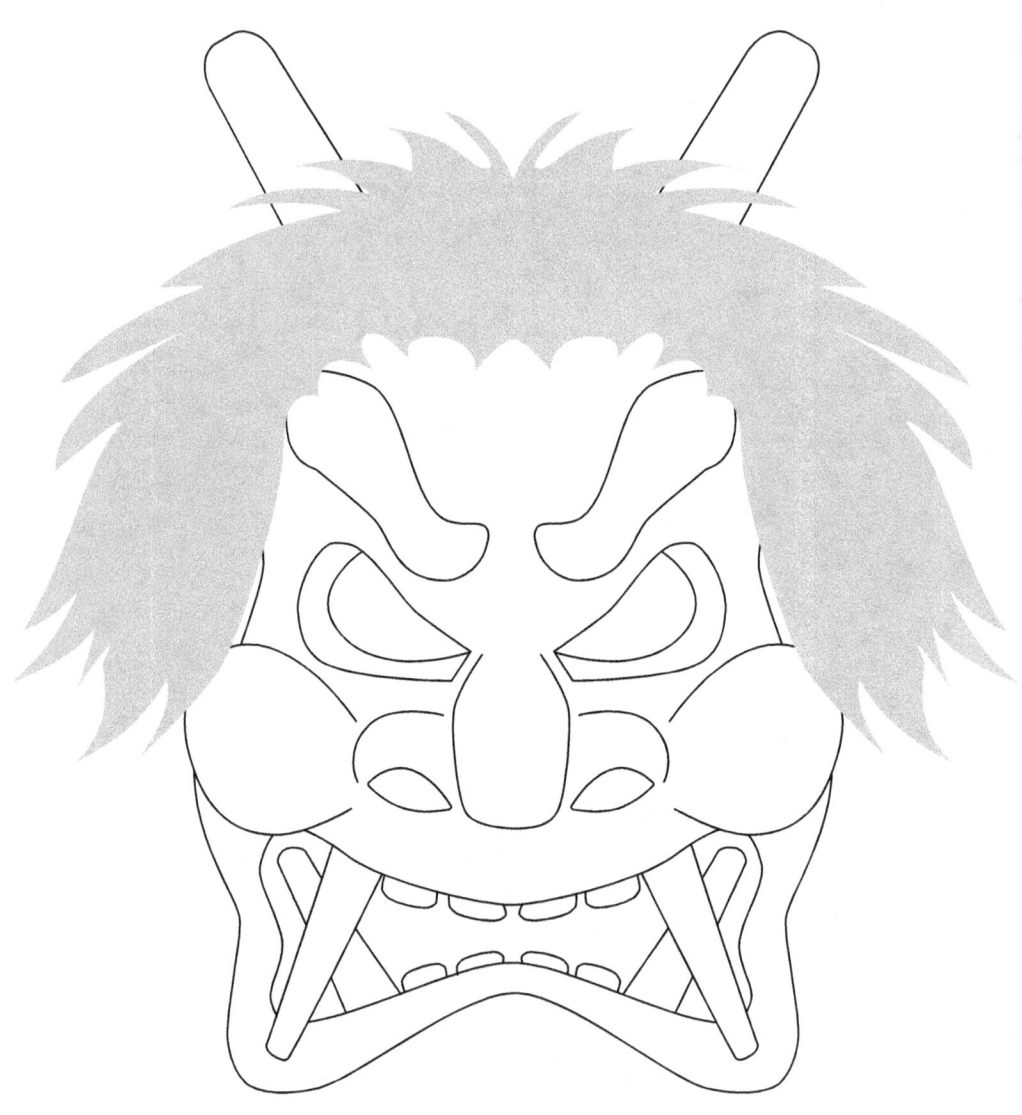

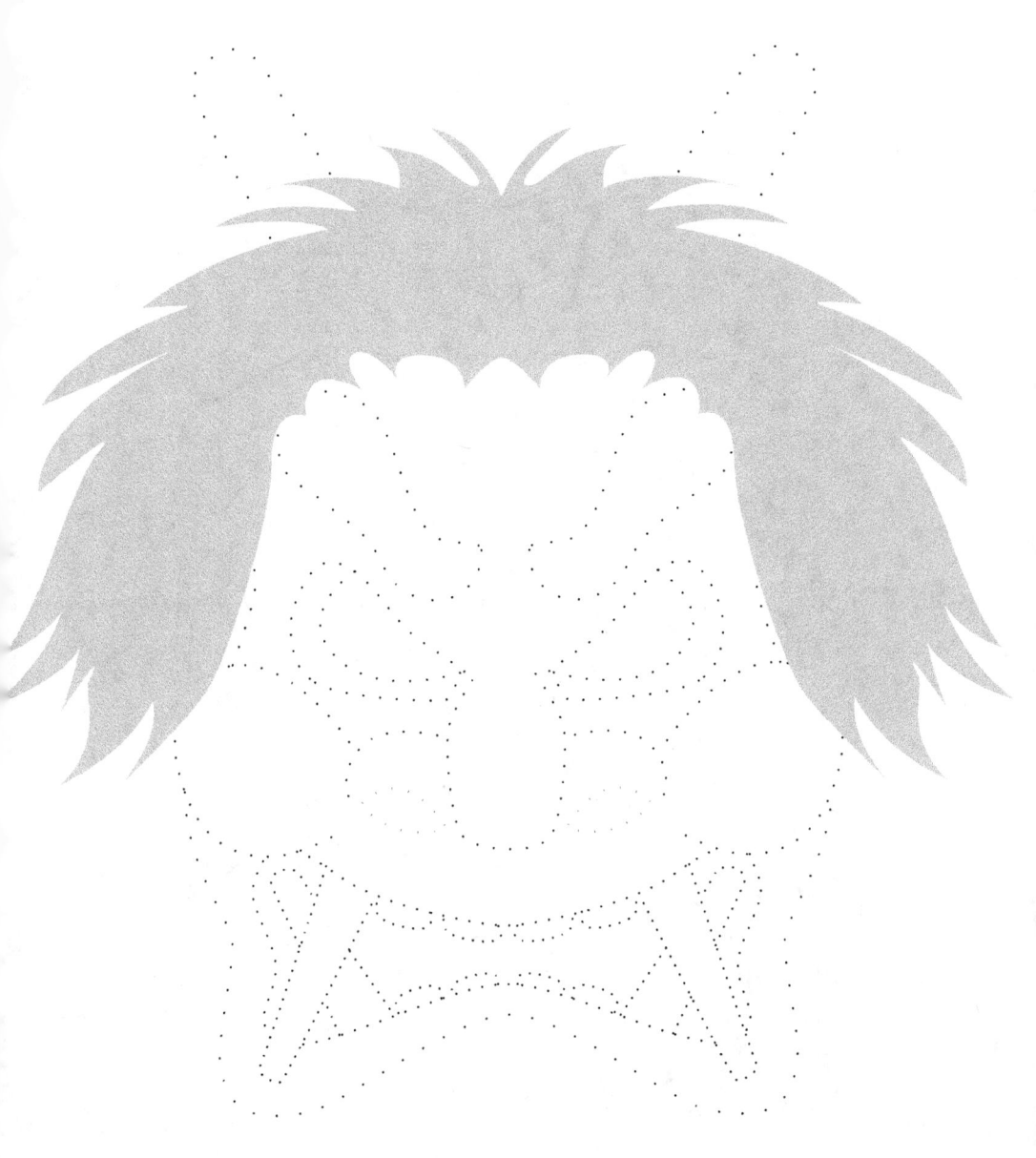

NWC Mask

Canada

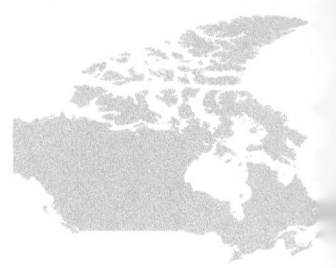

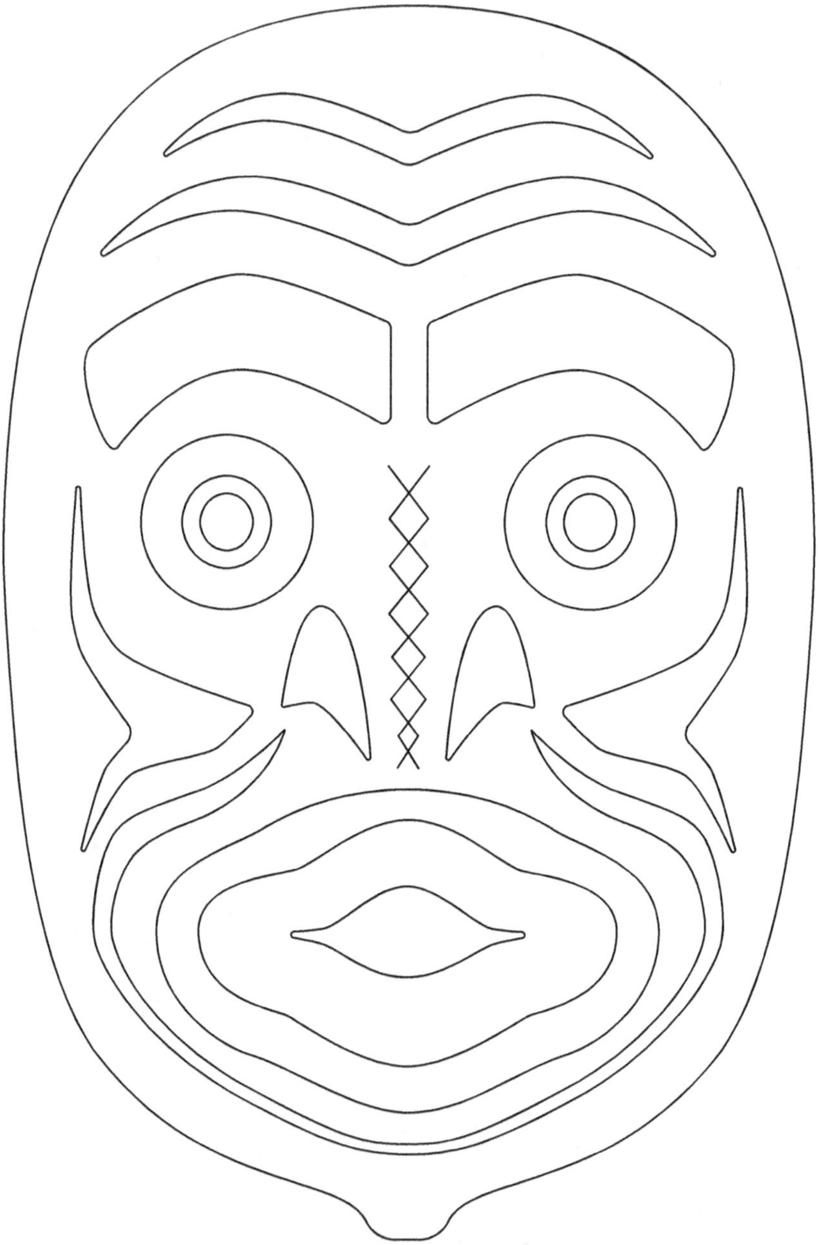

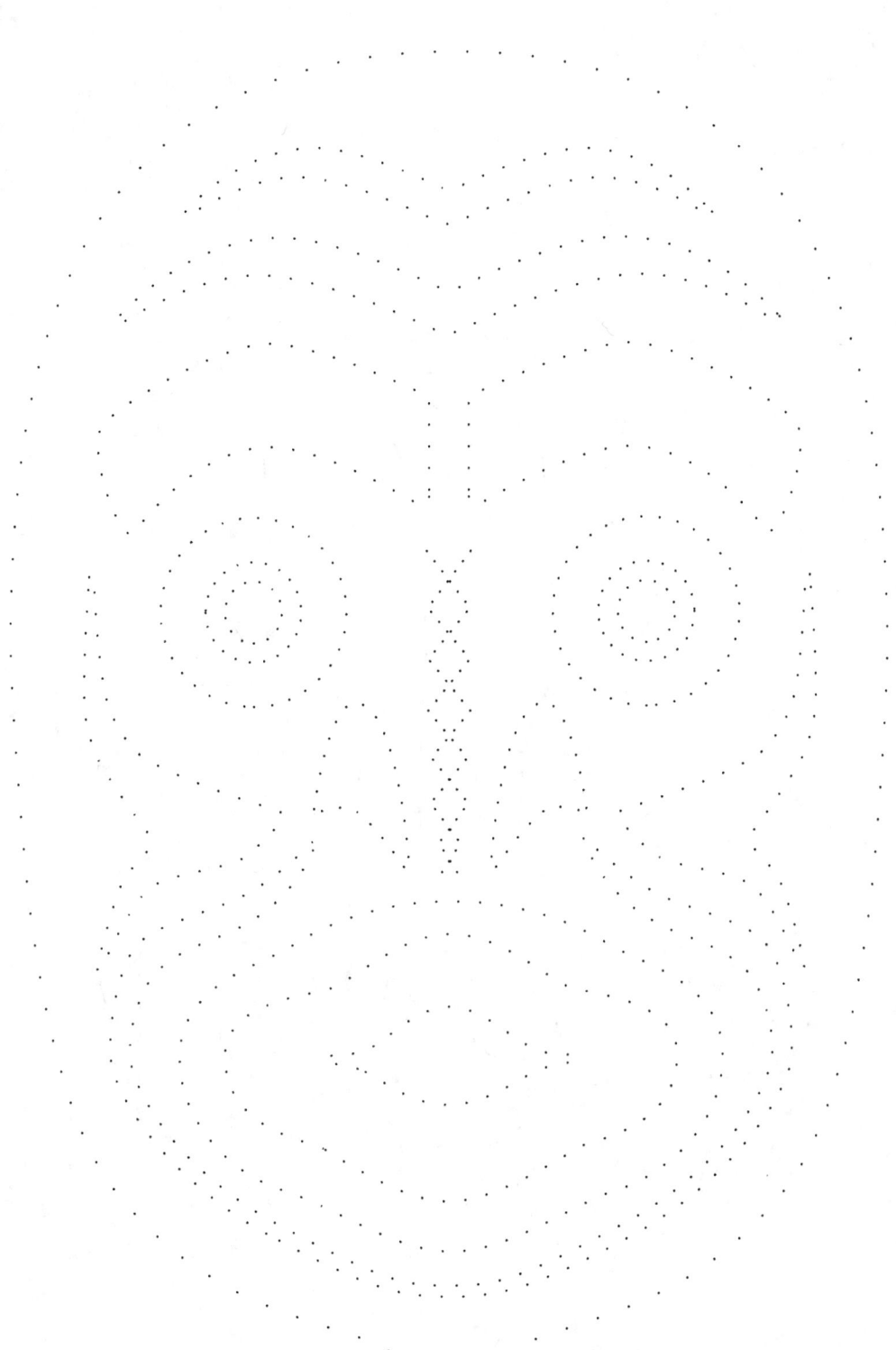

Opera Mask
China

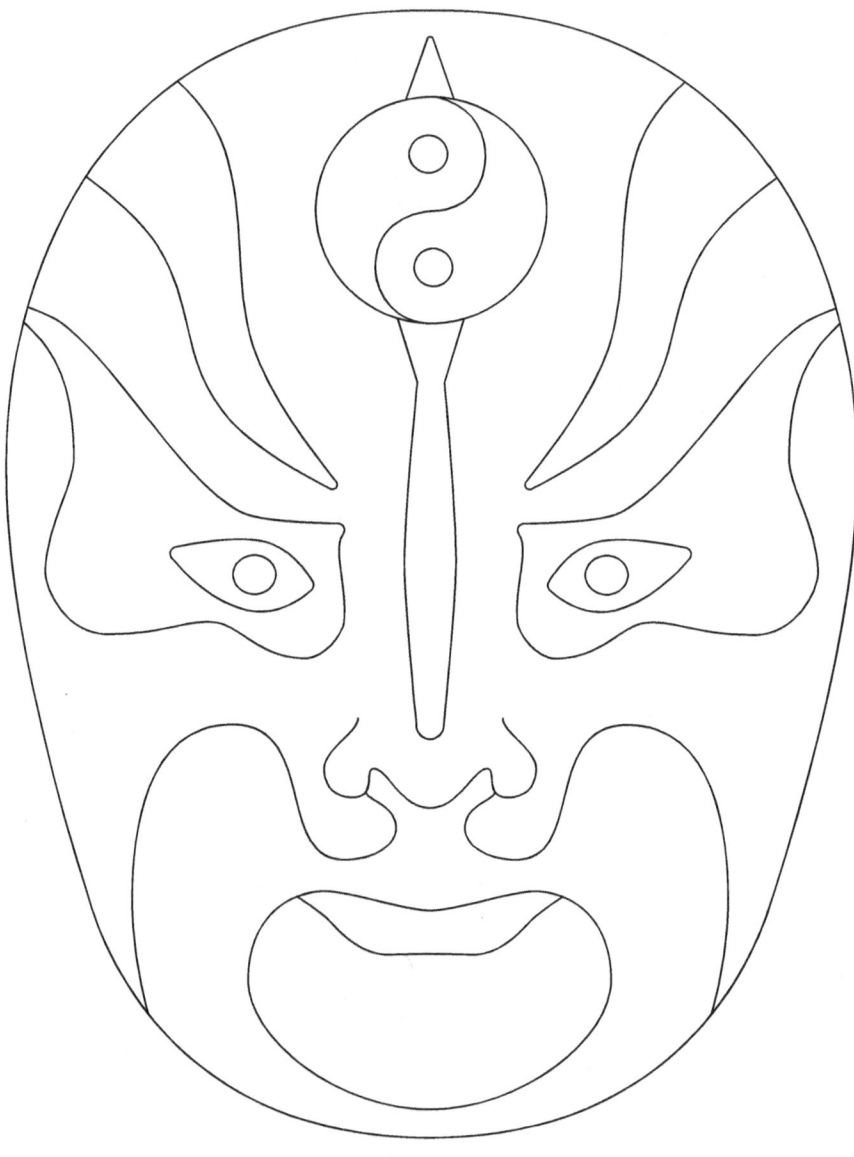

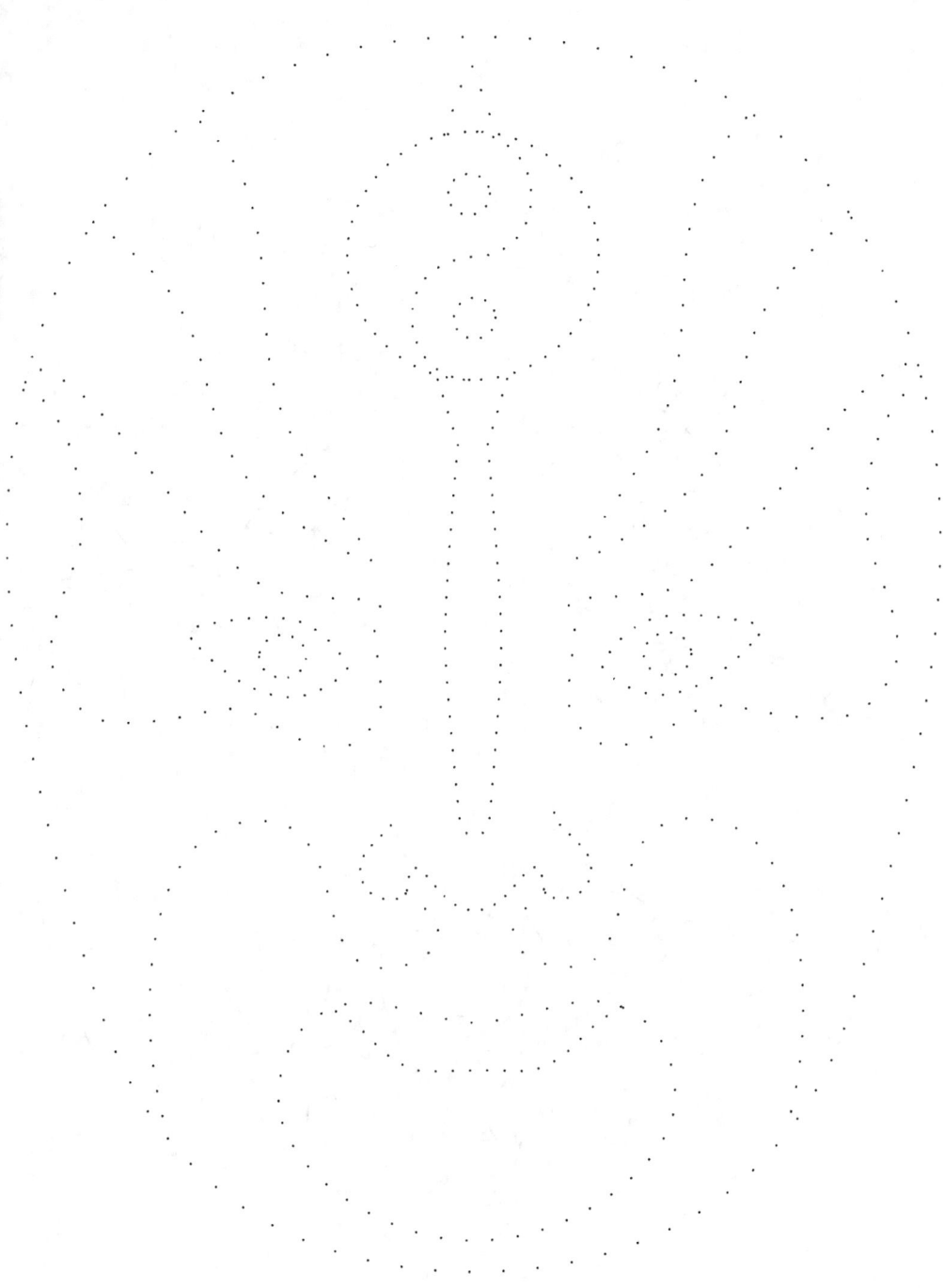

Owl Mask

Burkina Faso

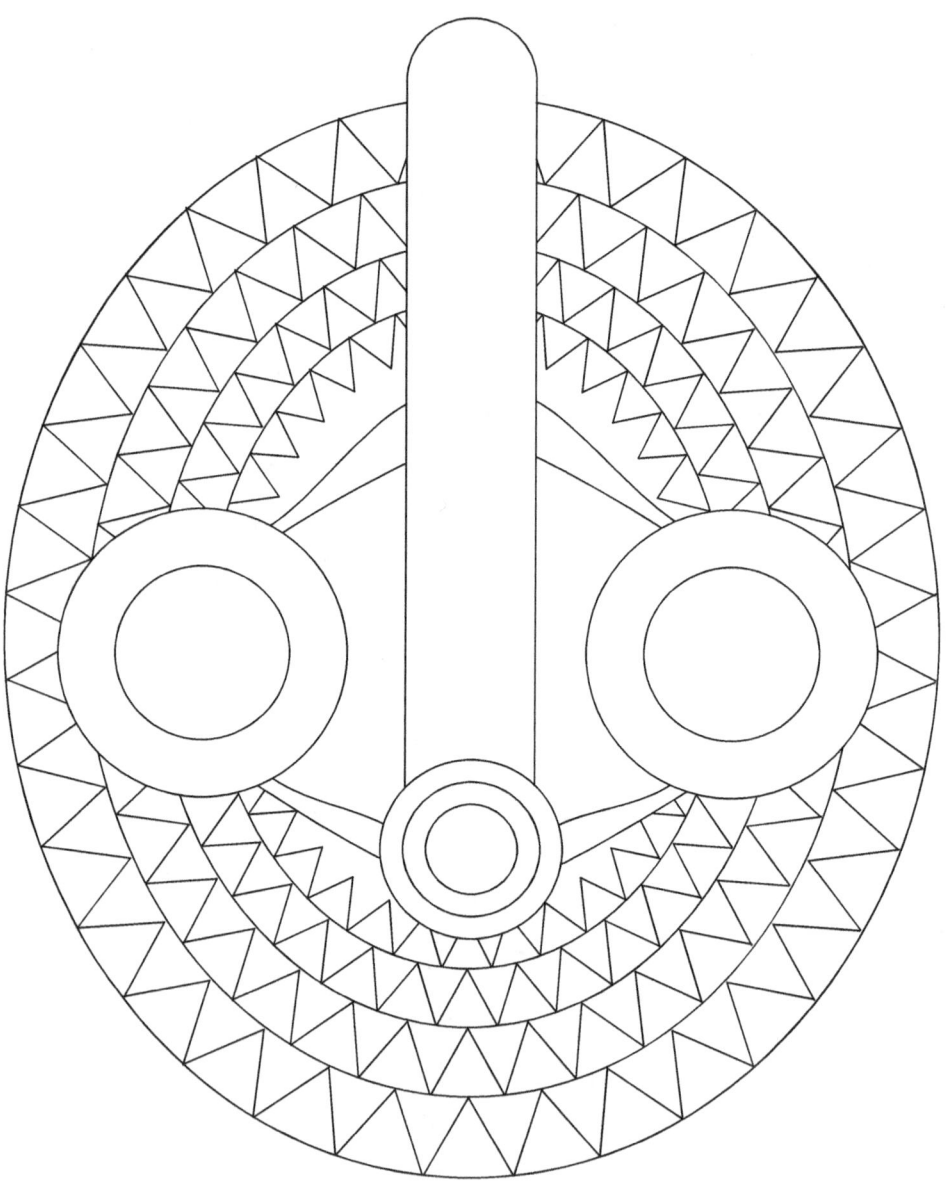

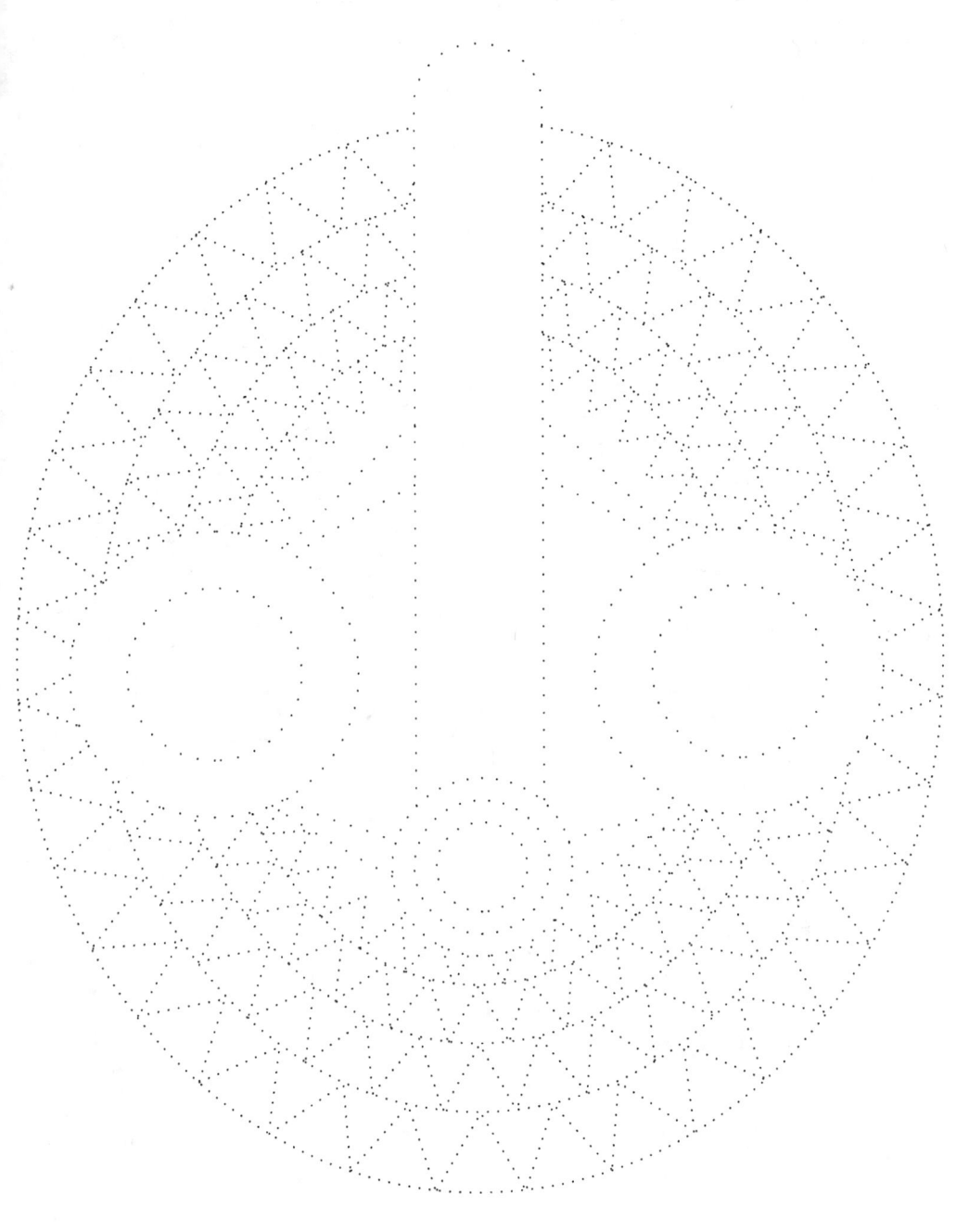

Pre-Columbian Mask

Mexico

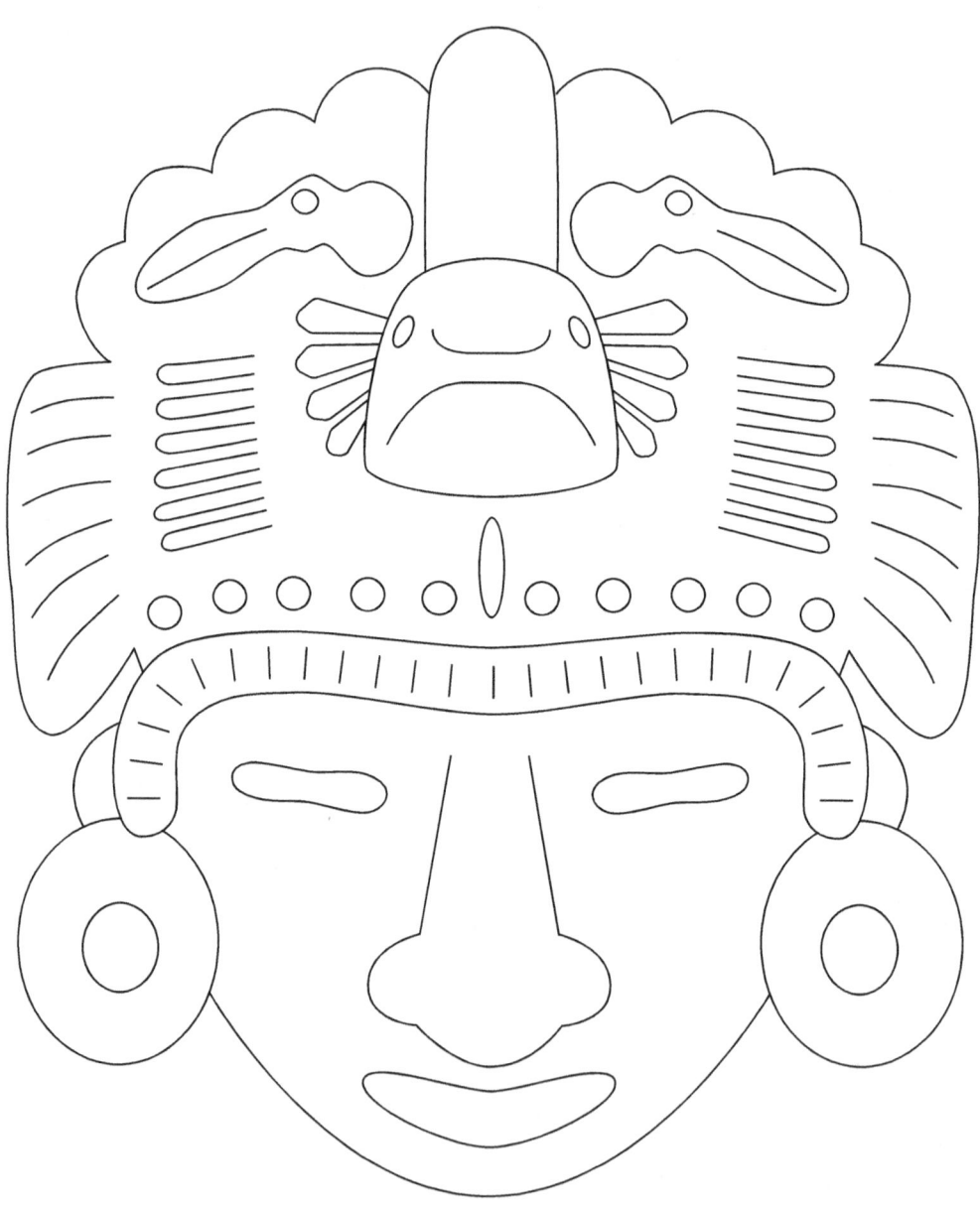

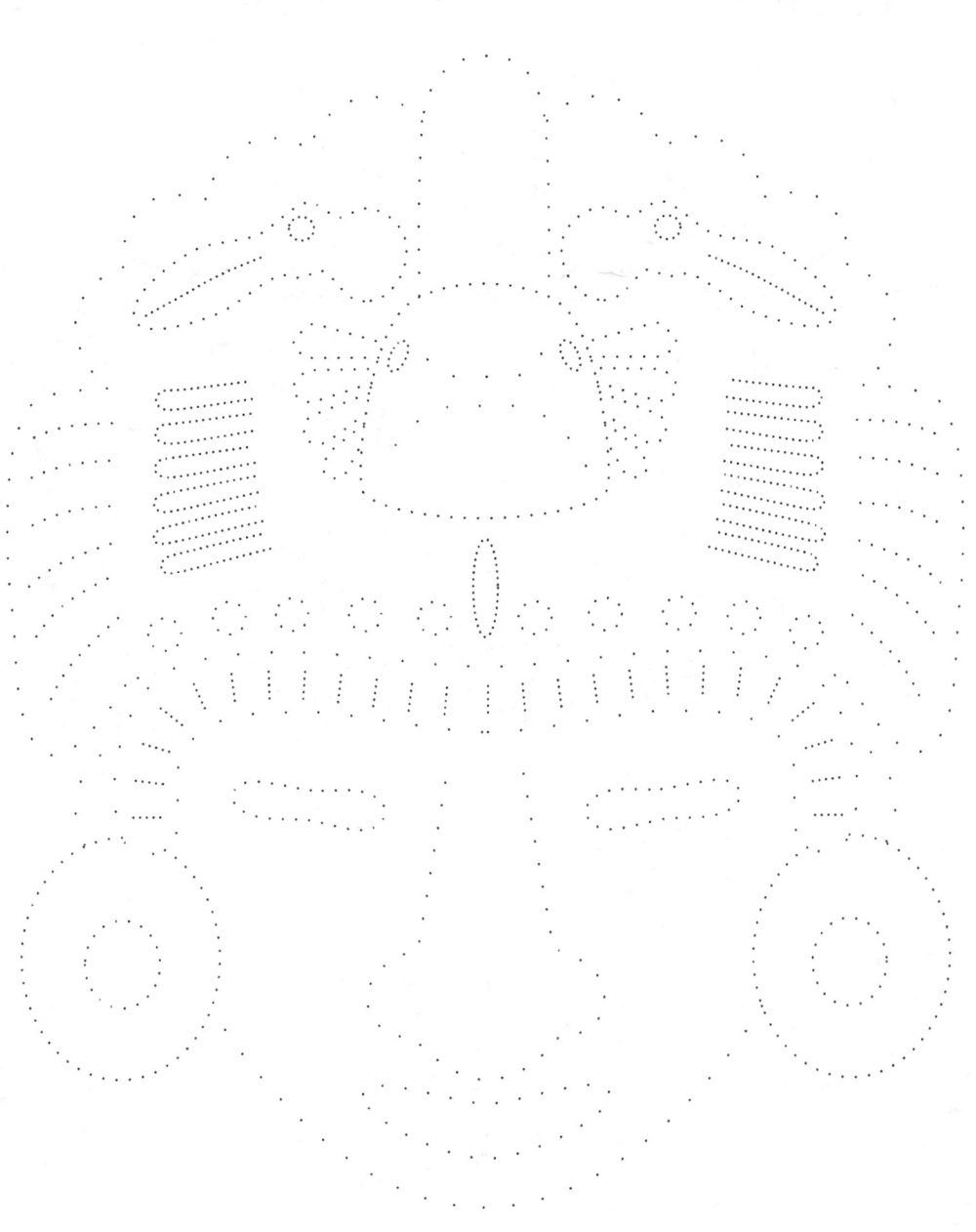

Rangda Mask

Bali, Indonesia

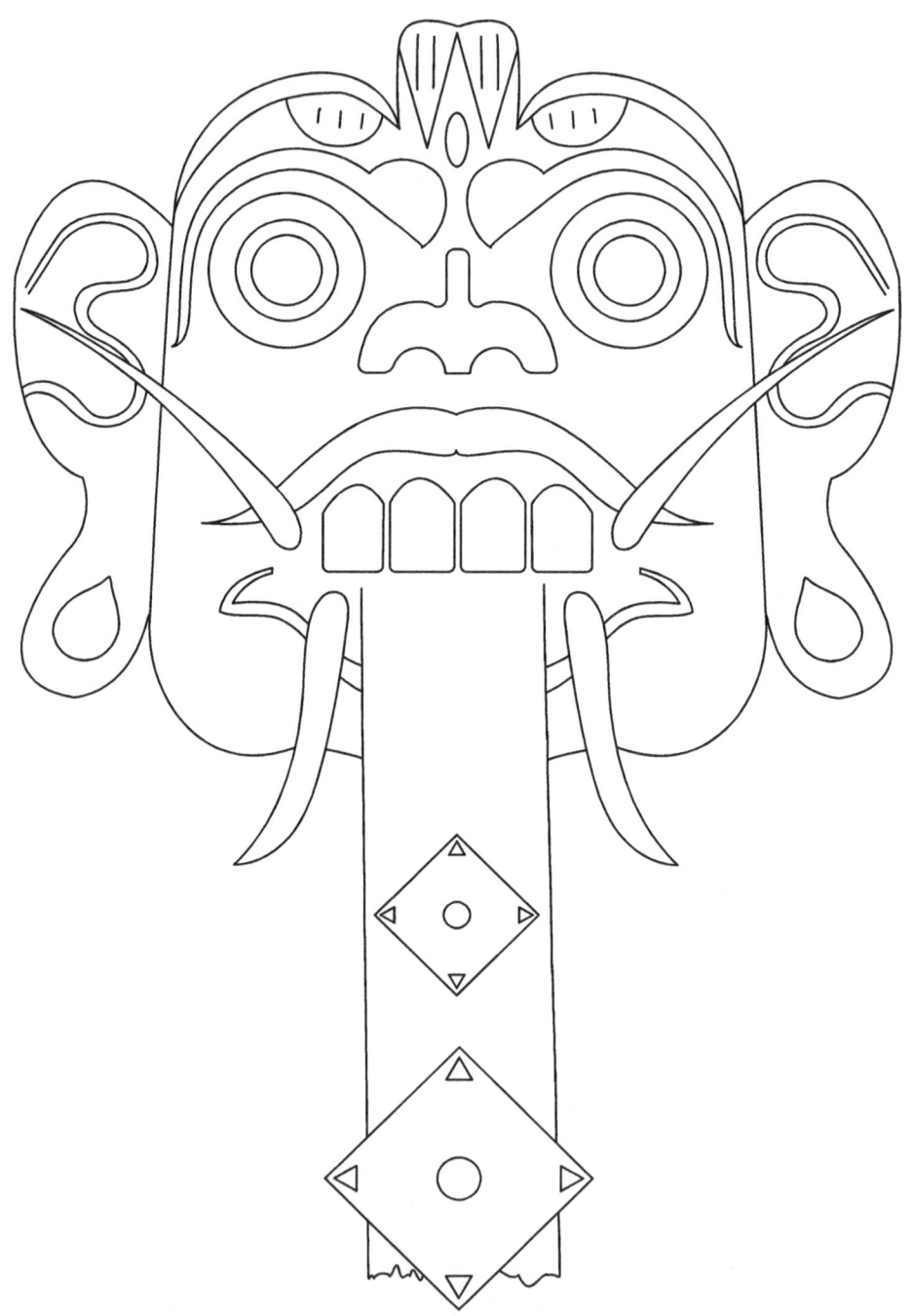

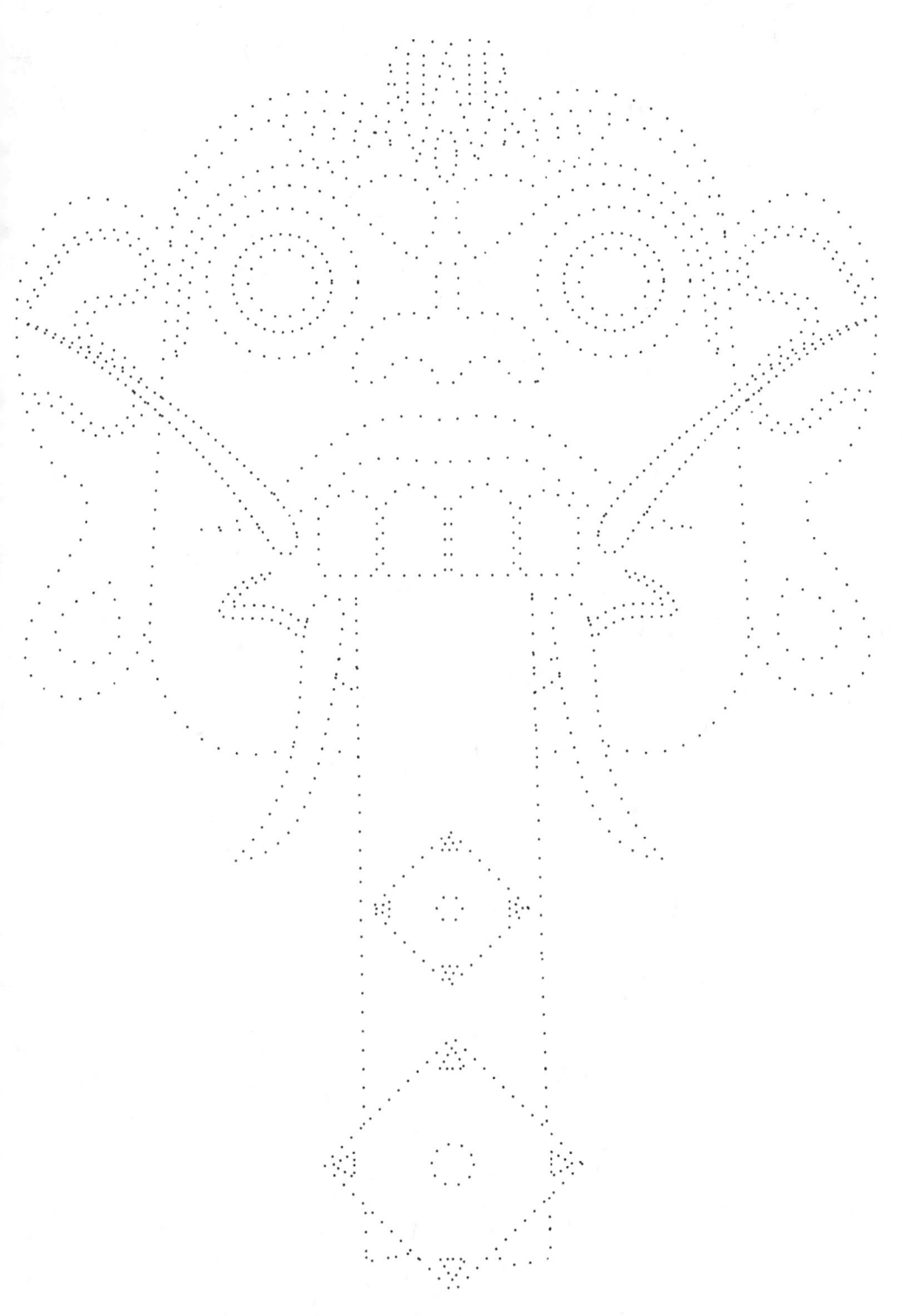

Tapuanu Mask

Mortlock Islands, Micronesia

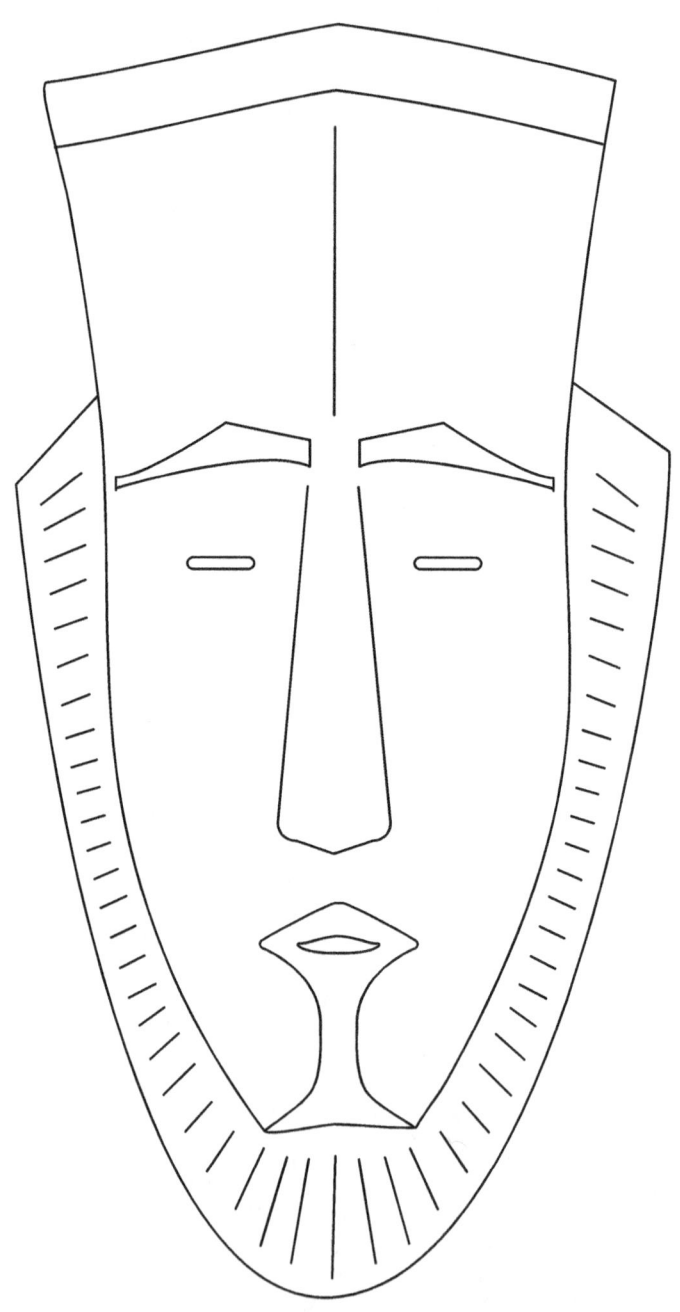

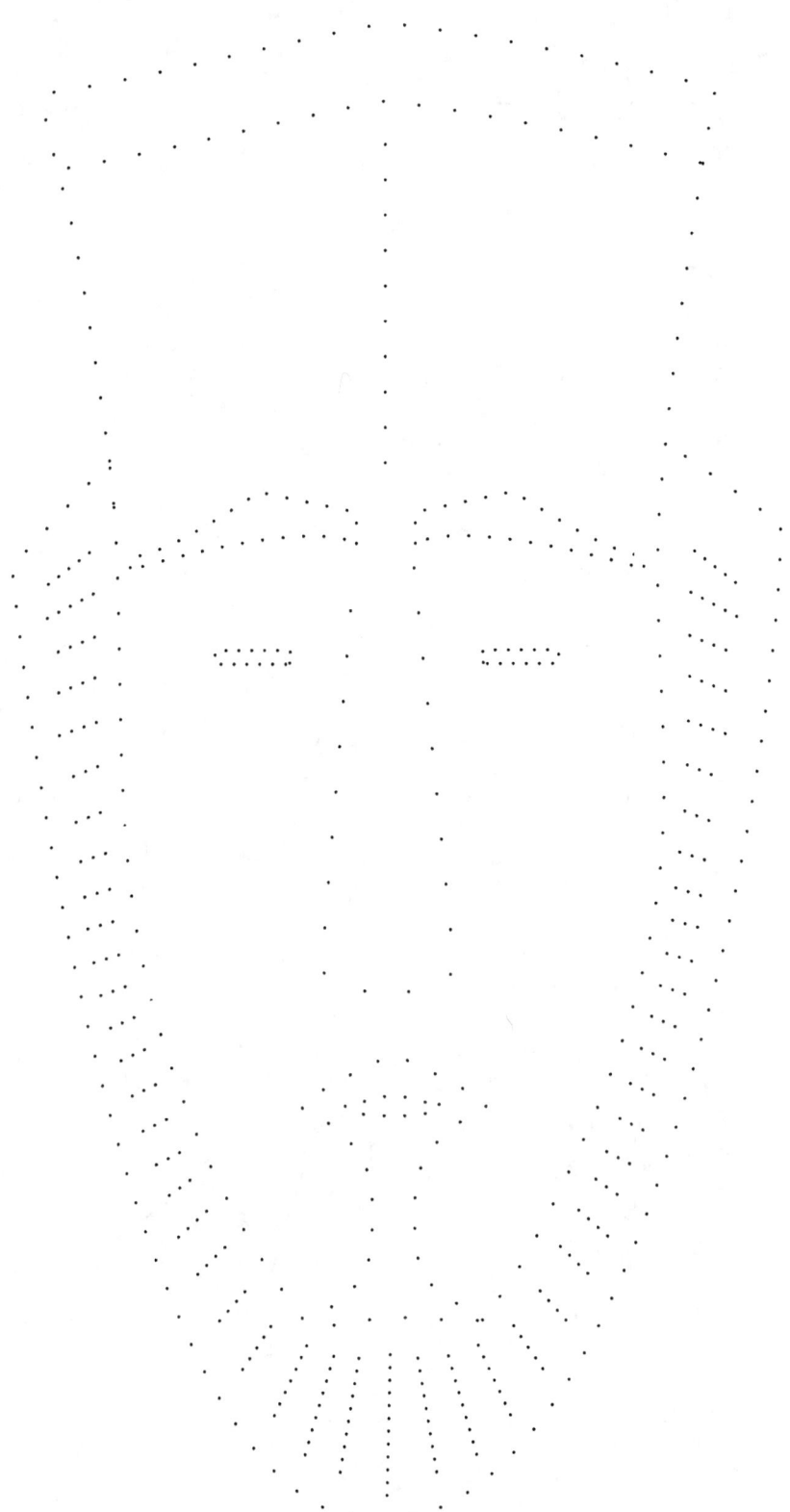

Tiger Mask

Mexico

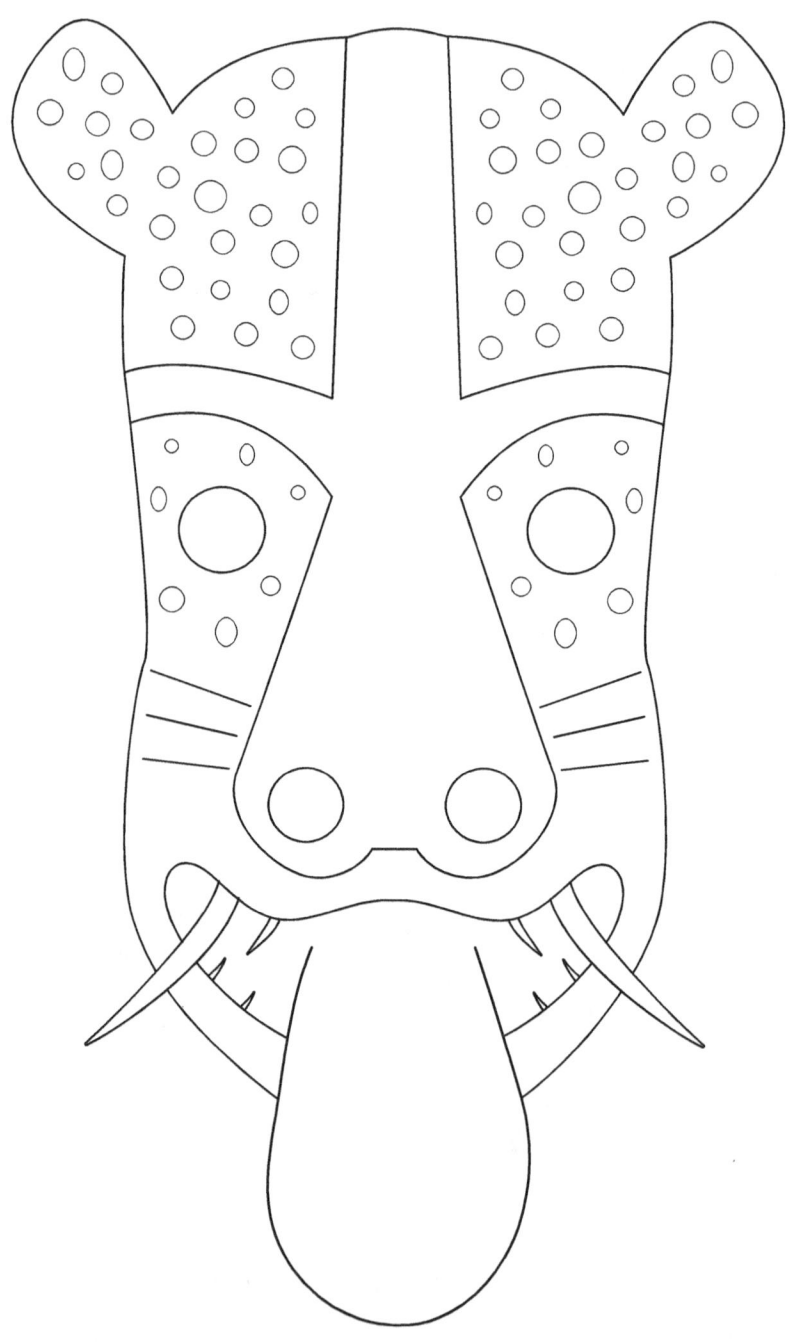

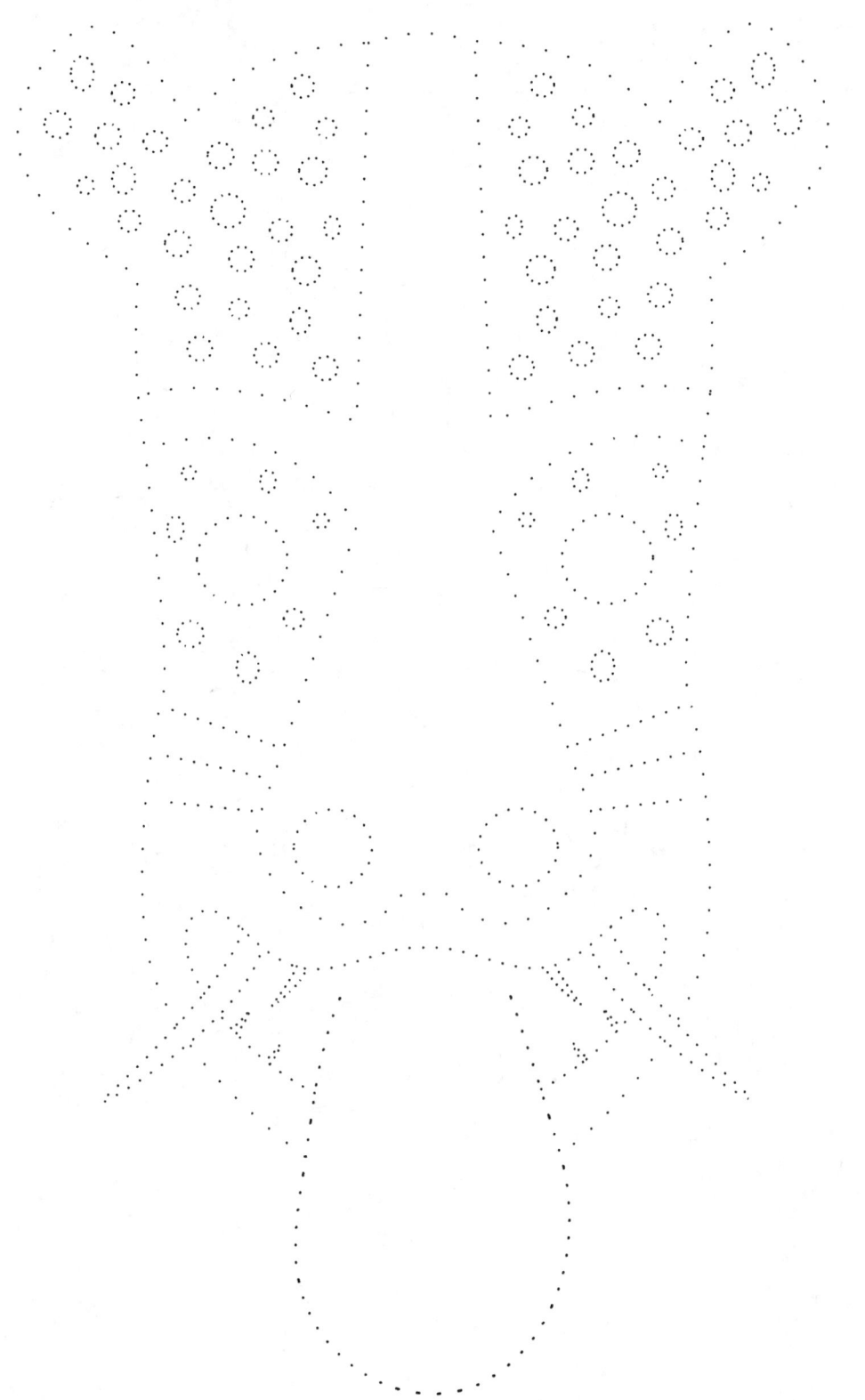

Tin Mask

Mexico

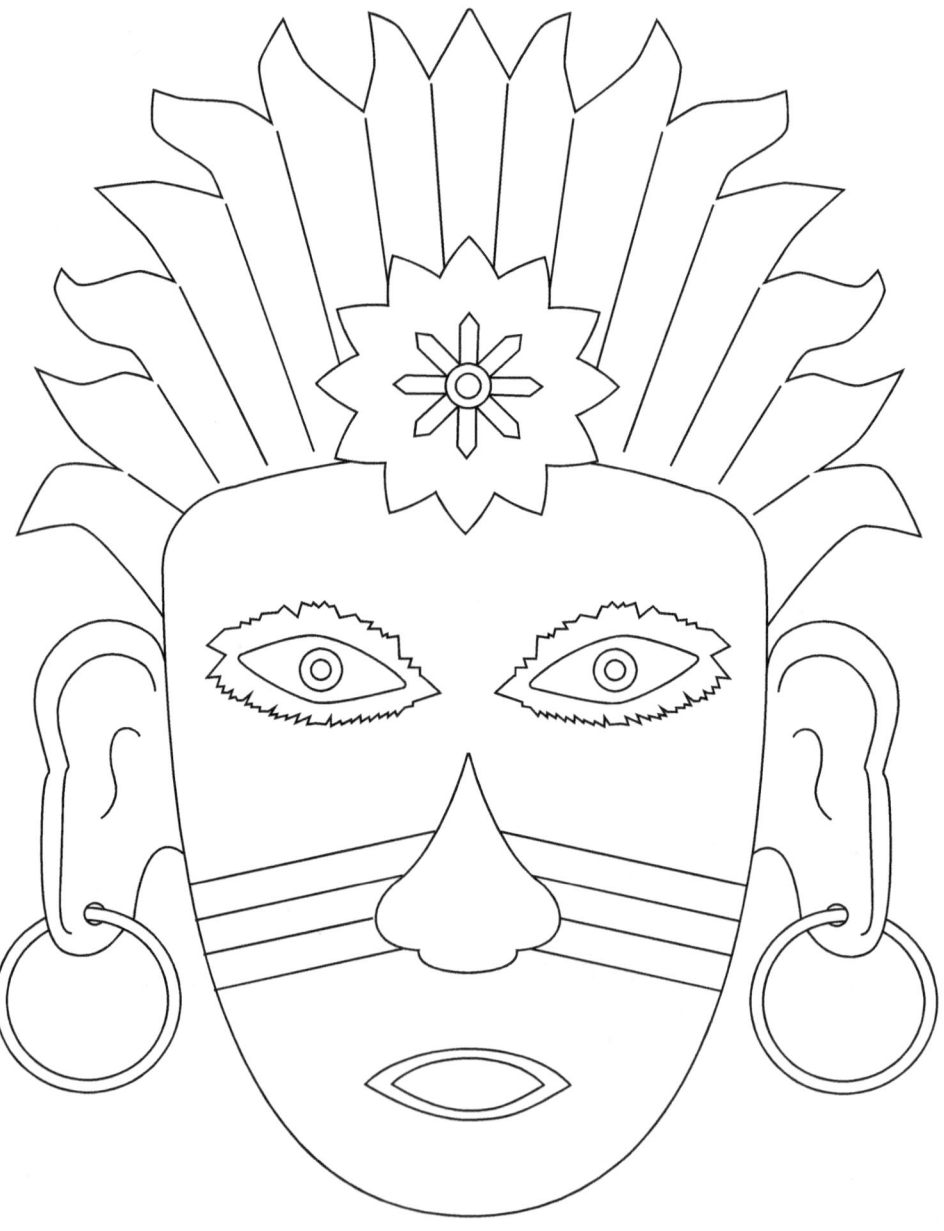

Venetian Mask

Italy

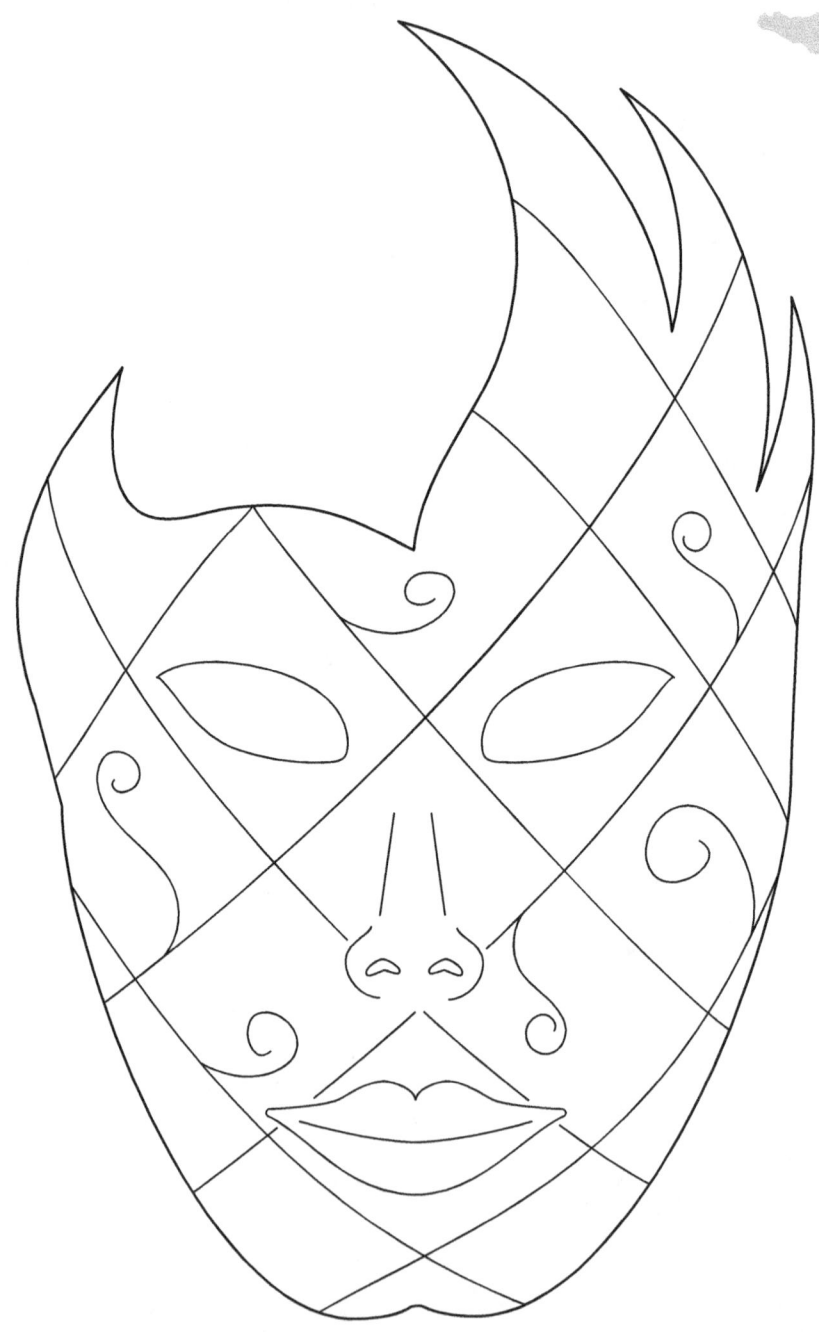

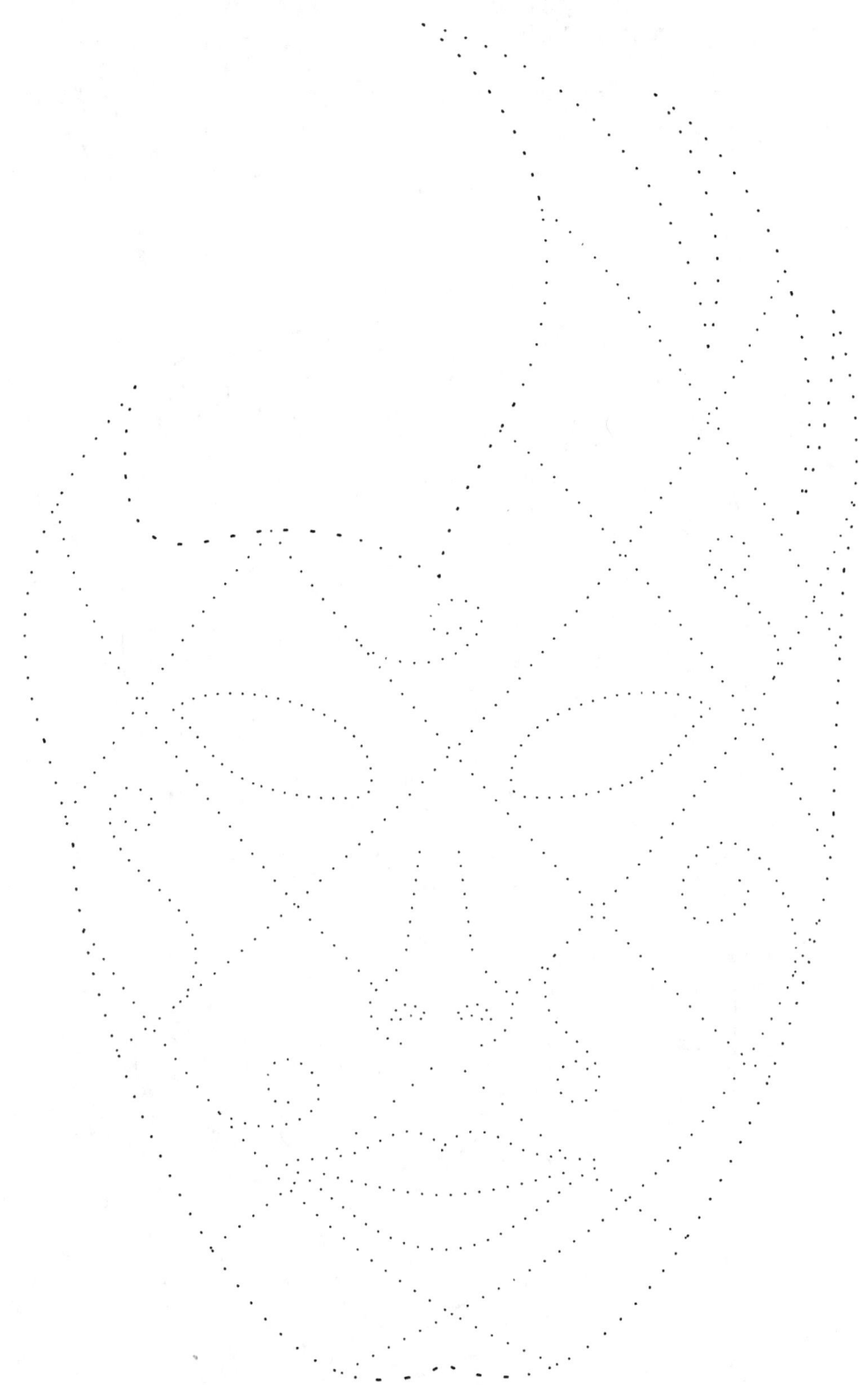

Warrior Mask
Kenya

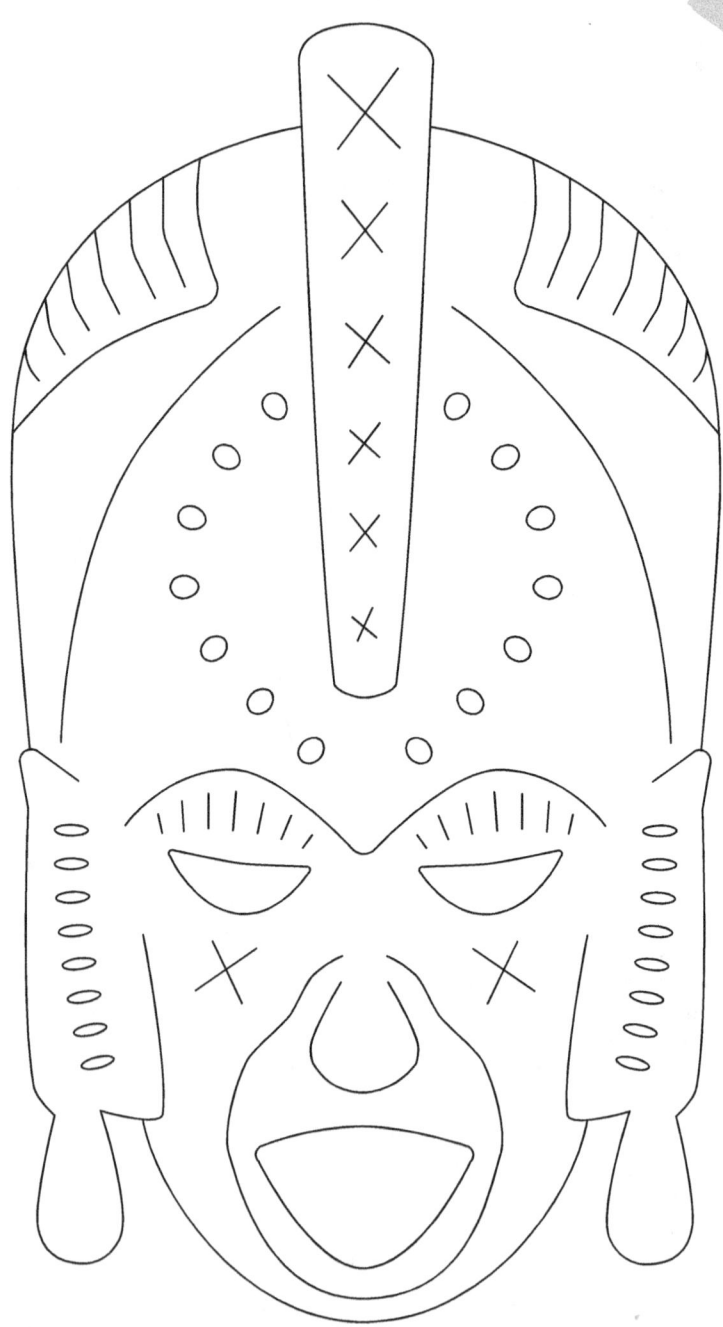

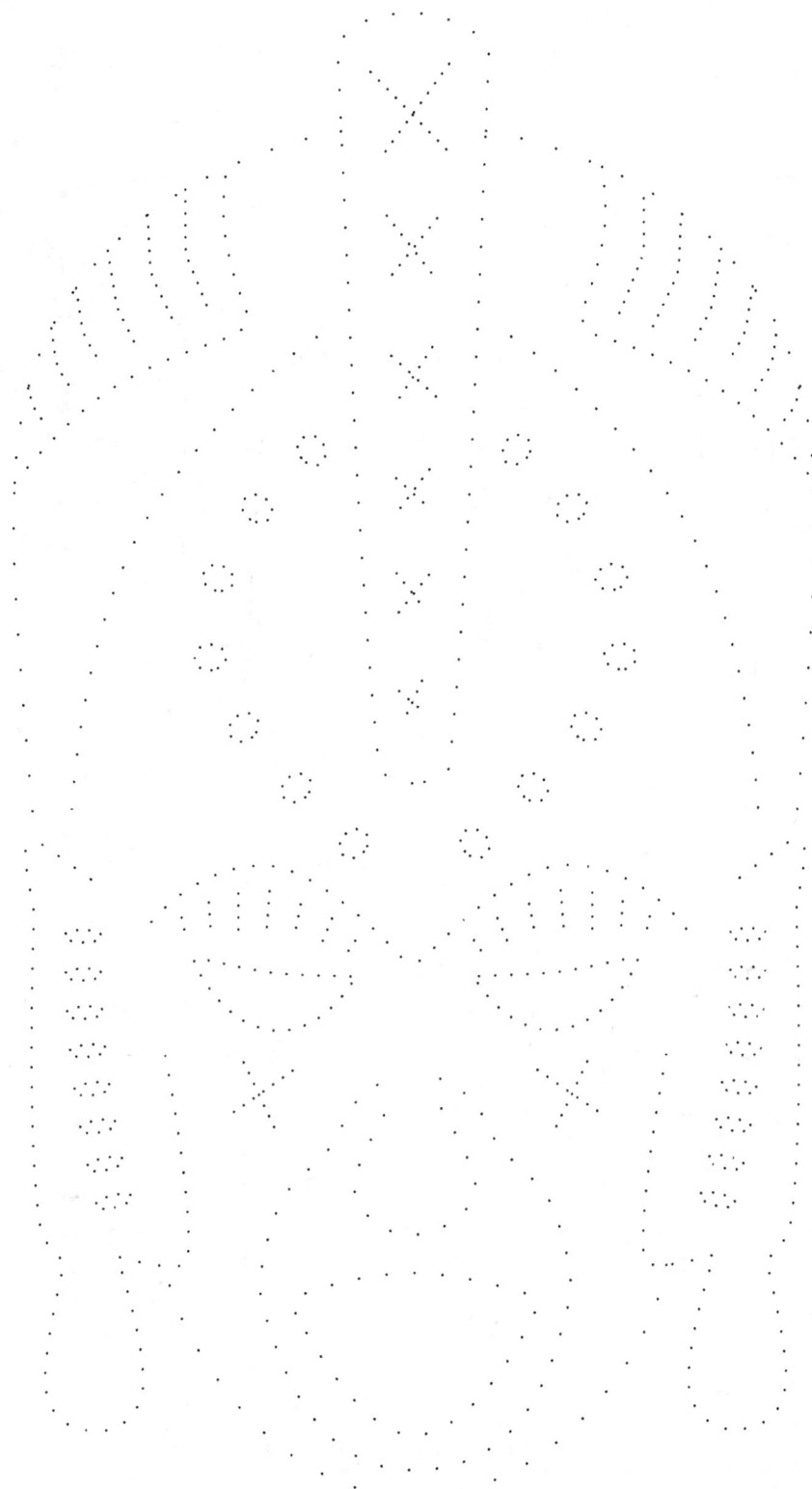

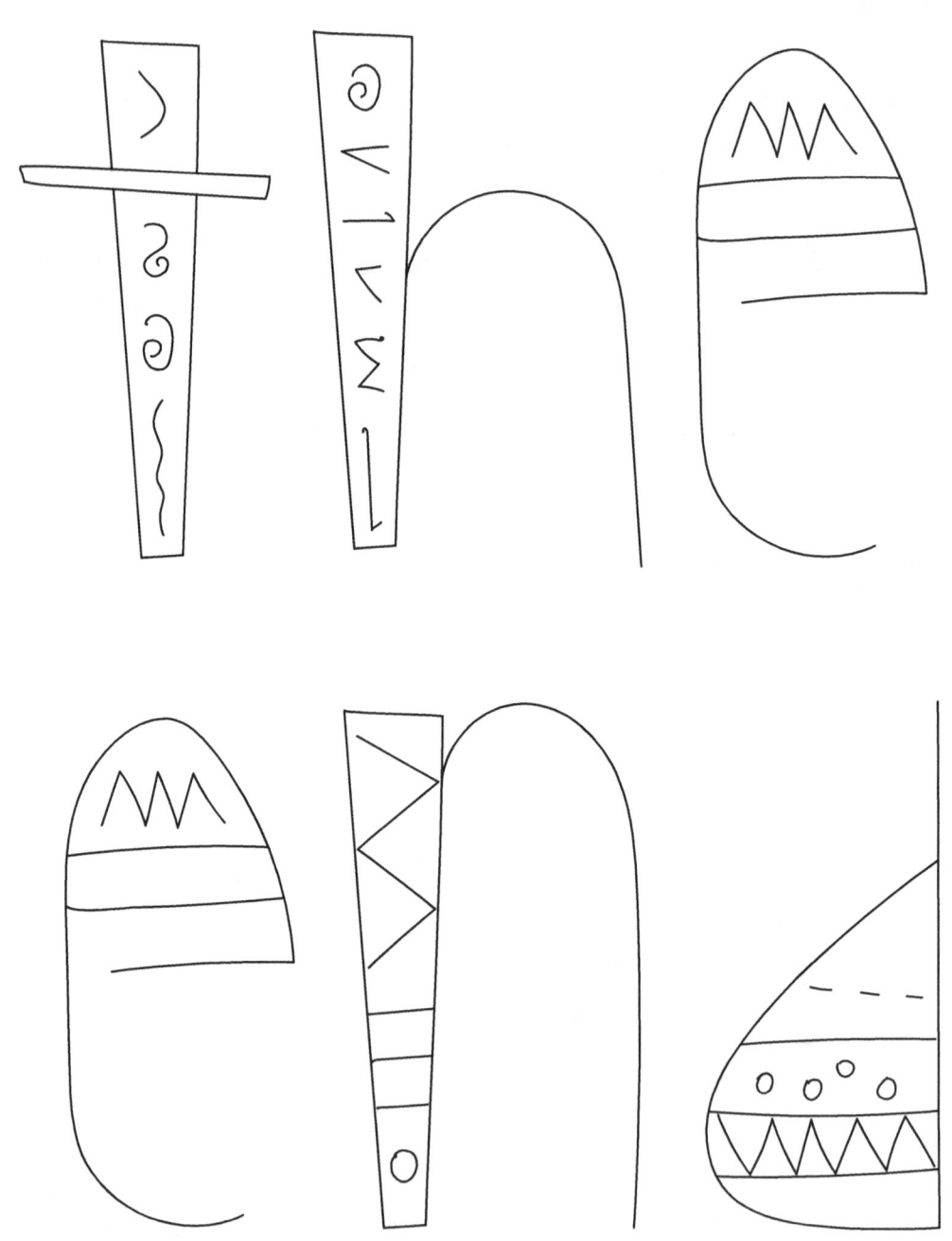

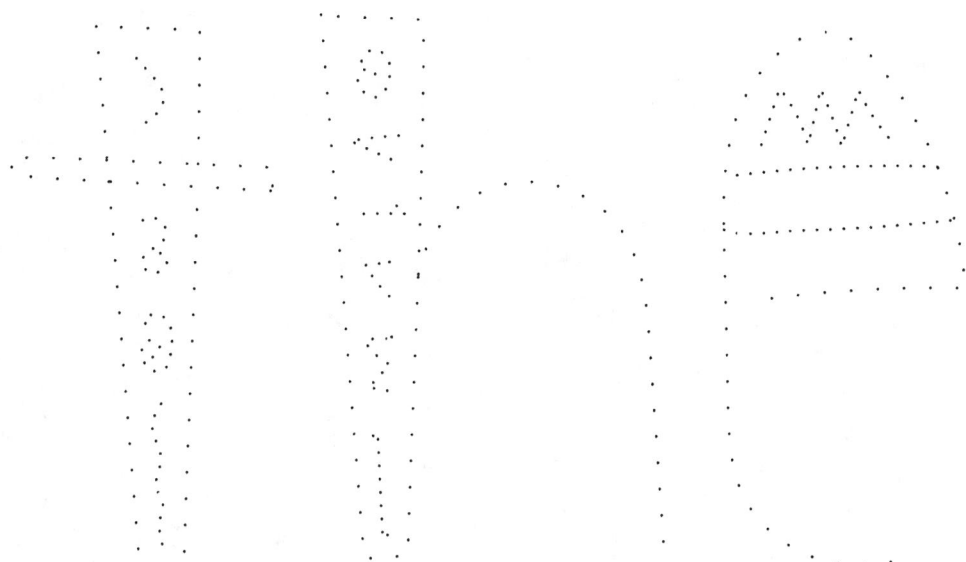
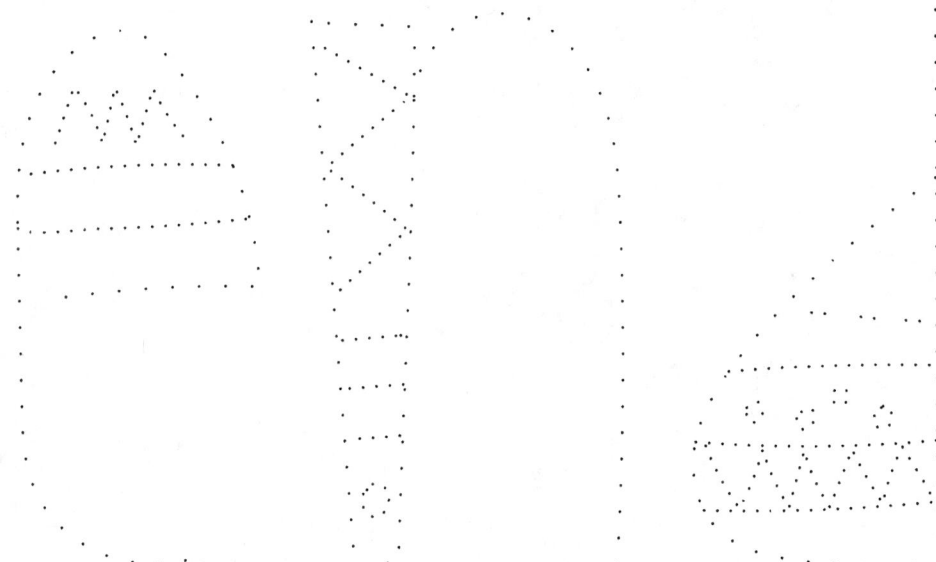

www.ingramcontent.com/pod-product-compliance
Lightning Source LLC
Chambersburg PA
CBHW071121240526

45465CB00022B/742